Awesome Worship Services for Youth

Group

Loveland, Colorado

Awesome Worship Services for Youth

Credits

Contributing Authors: Bob Buller, Stephanie Caro, Gary Glover, Lyle Griner, Mikal Keefer, Walter H. Mees Jr., Amy Simpson, and Arlo R. Reichter
Editors: Bob Buller and Michael D. Warden
Creative Development Editor: Dave Thornton
Chief Creative Officer: Joani Schultz
Copy Editor: Pamela Shoup
Designer and Art Director: Ray Tollison
Cover Art Director: Jeff A. Storm
Computer Graphic Artist: Nighthawk Design
Cover Designer/Illustrator: Jae Shim
Production Manager: Gingar Kunkel

Library of Congress Cataloging-in-Publication Data
Awesome worship services for youth.
     p.   cm.
   Includes index.
   ISBN 0-7644-2057-7
   1. Worship programs. 2. Church group work with youth. I. Group Publishing.
BV29.A94 1998
264'.00835–dc21

                       98-13277
                          CIP

10 9 8 7 6 5 4 3 2 1   07 06 05 04 03 02 01 00 99 98
Printed in the United States of America.

Contents

Contents

Introduction

If you're looking for innovative, awesome worship services for your youth group, you've come to the right place. Before you get into the nitty-gritty of the twelve worship programs contained in this book, let us tell you a little about the way the programs are designed. Several key characteristics make this book unique as a worship book for youth ministers:

● Each worship service contains four different forms of worship: celebration, reflection, symbolic action, and declaration. (More about this in a moment.)

● Each worship service is based on a biblical theme that describes who God is and what God has done. All of the worship activities in each service focus on the theme.

● These services provide a variety of traditional, contemporary, and innovative worship experiences, drawn from various Christian traditions. That way, young people will learn to appreciate worship in all of its expressions, and not just one or two.

Now, about the four worship forms included in each service: As you know, just as there are different styles of learning, there are different forms of worship. Because people are different, *Awesome Worship Services for Youth* includes each form of worship in every worship service. That means kids get to experience each of the following worship forms every time they worship:

● Celebration—This form of worship usually involves music and focuses on joyful expressions of praise.

● Reflection—This form of worship focuses on the inner experience of thoughtful praise. It involves silence, readings, dramas, and other thought-provoking experiences.

● Symbolic Action—This form of worship involves rituals that focus on the symbols of Christian faith. It might include re-enacting biblical events or creating symbols that express praise to God.

● Declaration—This form of worship focuses on committing our lives to God and declaring his truth. It may involve making bold statements of faith or committing to obey God's Word in daily life.

Even though each worship service contains all these elements, they do not all look alike. Some have several activities, while others have only a few. Sometimes the four worship forms are addressed separately. Other times they're combined in creative ways. The result? Each worship service is unique and provides kids with a powerful opportunity to worship God in creative and meaningful ways.

The main strength of these worship services is that they genuinely focus kids' attention on God. They guide young people to genuinely worship God—in ways that are often fun and non-threatening. They show them that in the process of subscribing worth to God, they will grow in their personal relationship with him. We trust that you'll be blessed as you experience these worship services with your youth group or perhaps even with your entire church.

The Lord Who Is Worthy of Praise

Worship Themes:
God is worthy of our worship.
We should worship God in spirit and truth.

Worship Scriptures:
1 Chronicles 16:23-25; Psalms 18:1-3, 28; 28:7; 95:1; 145:3-9; John 4:24; and John 6:35

Worship Overview:
Jesus taught us that we must worship God in spirit and in truth (John 4:24). Worshiping God in spirit means that our spirits should draw close to and commune with God's Spirit during worship. When we truly worship God, we're not merely repeating pious platitudes or singing sacred songs. We are entering into the real, spiritual presence of God.

Worshiping God in truth requires us to honor God for who he really is in a way that is also true to who we are. Our worship pleases God most when we offer thanks and adoration in a way that reflects who we truly are.

This service will help your kids experience the kind of authentic worship that pleases God. Use the worship experiences that follow to help your kids truly worship God for who he is and for what he has done in their lives.

Supply Checklist

- Bibles
- index cards
- a softball-size rock (or larger)
- a lantern or flashlight
- paper
- a shield (or a picture of a shield)   *will a bullet-proof vest work?*
- an uncut loaf of bread
- pencils or markers

Worship Preparation:
Before the service, select several worship songs to sing during the "Opening Celebration."

Review the "Standing in the Presence of God" reading (pp. 12-13) until you are familiar enough with it to read it dramatically. If you'd like, create a soundtrack to go along with the reading. (See the Leader Tip on page 8.)

Set the rock, shield, lantern or flashlight, and uncut loaf of bread where they can be quickly retrieved. Place the paper and the pencils or markers nearby.

Worship Service

Opening Celebration

God Is Worthy of Worship

(10 minutes)

Begin the worship service by leading the group in several praise or worship songs that group members are likely to know. Encourage kids to praise God freely, expressing themselves in whatever way they feel comfortable, as they sing songs such as the following.

- "I Will Enter His Gates"
- "Awesome God"
- "Father, I Adore You"
- "Lord, I Lift Your Name on High"
- "Thou Art Worthy"

After five minutes of singing, ask kids to reflect on what they just sang and experienced. Have kids form groups of three or four. Then have kids silently answer the following questions. After asking each question, allow kids thirty seconds of reflection time and then encourage kids to share their answers with group members. Ask:

- **How were you worshiping God while we were singing?**
- **What do you think it means to genuinely worship God?**
- **When is worship meaningful for you? not meaningful?**
- **When is worship meaningful for God? not meaningful?**

Ask for several volunteers to report their group's answers, then say: **True worship requires at least two things: a genuine awareness that we are in the presence of God and a genuine expression of what we think or feel about God. Of course, since we're all different, there may be many ways we can each truly worship God. But no matter what style of worship we prefer, our worship should always make us realize that we are in the presence of God, and that he is worthy of our praise. Let's spend several minutes imagining what it would feel like to actually be in God's presence.**

Worshipful Reflection

Standing in the Presence of God

(15 minutes)

Invite kids to find a comfortable and private place to sit or to recline, preferably away from any distractions and outside noises. Then read the "Standing in the Presence of God" reflection (pp. 12-13).

After the reflection, lead the group in singing the same worship or praise songs you sang earlier. Encourage kids to sing thoughtfully as they worship, remembering that they actually are in the presence of God.

After singing several songs, ask the group:

- **Was this worship experience different from the one earlier? Why or why not?**

Leader Tip

To heighten the realism of this experience, make a soundtrack to go along with the reading. You might record the entire reading on tape or supplement your own reading with recorded special effects such as the divine voice, thunder, lightning, a choir repeating the angelic chants, or even "The Hallelujah Chorus" from Handel's *Messiah*.

Next, ask for volunteers to read aloud 1 Chronicles 16:23-25; Psalms 18:1-3; and 145:3-9. Then have kids re-form their original groups of three or four and discuss the following questions. After each question, ask volunteers to report each group's answers. Ask:

● **What do these Scriptures teach us about why God is worthy of worship?**

● **What do the songs we sang teach us about why God is worthy of worship?**

● **How can remembering we are in God's presence give our worship meaning?**

Say: **When we worship God, we need to remember that we are not simply singing songs or repeating words. Rather, we are standing in the presence of the one true God, the only one who is worthy of our worship. Let's spend a few moments telling God why we think he is worthy of our worship.**

Instruct kids to spend one to two minutes in silent prayer, telling God specifically why he is worthy of their worship. Remind kids that they are actually in the presence of God, and encourage kids to name specific reasons that God is worthy of their worship.

After a few minutes, close by praying: **God, we acknowledge that you are worthy of our worship both for who you are and for what you have done for us. You are a great and awesome God, but you invite us to enter your presence. You are a holy God who cannot even look upon sin, but you forgive our sins so we can stand in your presence and worship you. For all that you are, God, we worship you. For all that you have done for us, we worship and thank you. Be with us as we continue to worship you, our great and loving God. In Jesus' name, amen.**

"God is spirit, and his worshipers must worship in spirit and in truth."
—John 4:24

Symbolic Declaration

Concrete Reminders of Abstract Truths

(25 minutes)

Say: **True worship begins when we enter into the presence of God. But what should we do once we are there? Let's take a look at God's Word to see how God wants us to worship once we have entered into the presence of God.**

Have a volunteer read aloud John 4:24. Then ask the entire group the following questions.

Encourage them to share their responses as a way of declaring God's character with the whole group.

- **What do you think it means to worship God in spirit?**
- **What do you think it means to worship God in truth?**

Say: **We worship God in spirit by entering God's presence to spend time with him, our spirit with his Spirit. We worship God in truth by praising God in a way that is true to ourselves and to who God is. Of course, because God is Spirit, sometimes it's difficult to grasp who he really is. That's why the Bible uses symbols to help us understand and worship God for who he is.**

Hold up the rock, and ask for a volunteer to read aloud Psalm 95:1. Then ask the entire group the following questions. Once again, encourage them to share their responses with the whole group.

- **In what ways do you think God is a rock to his people?**
- **What characteristics of a rock are also true of God?**
- **In what specific ways has God been a rock in your life?**

Encourage kids to pray silently for thirty seconds, thanking God for being a rock in their lives.

After thirty seconds, say "amen." Hold up the shield, and have a volunteer read aloud Psalm 28:7. Then ask the entire group the same three questions, substituting the word "shield" for "rock." Give kids thirty seconds to thank God for being a shield in their lives. Repeat the process with a lantern or flashlight (Psalm 18:28) and an uncut loaf of bread (John 6:35).

Then give each person a sheet of paper and a pencil or marker. Ask kids to silently consider what symbol or image comes to mind when they think of God. After a minute, instruct kids to draw the symbol on the sheet of paper. Encourage kids to draw a symbol that is true for them. For example, someone might draw an airplane because God takes them to great heights, a lighthouse that always brings them in safely, or a wonderful book that has answers to all their questions. Tell kids they have three minutes to work. Then they will take turns displaying and explaining their symbols. While kids are working on their symbols, draw your own.

After three minutes, have kids form a circle. Hold up your picture, and complete the following sentence: **I worship you, God, because you are a** (symbol) **that** (explanation). For example, you might state, "I worship you, God, because you are a safe, warm home that protects me from the cold winds of life." Then have kids take turns completing the sentence as they display their pictures.

Leader Tip

If you cannot find any of the objects, substitute pictures of them. If you are short of time, eliminate one or two symbols. If you want to extend or modify this worship experience, use a shepherd's staff (Psalm 23:1) or a crown (Psalm 47:2).

"I call to the Lord, who is worthy of praise, and I am saved from my enemies." —Psalm 18:3

When everyone has displayed his or her symbol, say: **Look around the room and observe all the different reasons God is worthy of our worship. God is far greater than any one person's ideas about him. So when we worship God, let's remember that we need to worship God in spirit—with the attitude that we are truly in his presence—and in truth, for who he really is.**

Closing Commitment

Personal Expressions of Worship
(5 minutes)

Say: **During our worship service, we have worshiped God in spirit and in truth. We have entered into his awesome presence and praised him for who he truly is. But worship isn't something that we should do only at special times or in special ways. God wants us to worship him at various times and in various ways.**

Briefly explain to kids that they can worship God at any time and in any way that truly expresses their adoration of God. Spend a few minutes introducing the four worship forms—celebrative, reflective, symbolic, and declarative—discussed in the Introduction to this book. Then ask kids to discuss the following questions with their original group members. Ask:

● **What part of our worship service was most meaningful to you?**
● **What does this reveal about the way you prefer to worship God?**

Distribute one index card to each student. Instruct kids to each write on their index cards one way they will worship God in their preferred way during the next week. Allow kids several minutes to write out their ideas, then encourage group members to close in prayer, thanking God for the privilege of worshiping him and committing themselves to worship him during the coming week.

Standing in the Presence of God

Either read or retell in your own words the following description of what it would be like to enter into God's heavenly presence. Be sure to read or tell the descriptions slowly—allowing kids adequate time to imagine the scenes you describe.

Close your eyes, and imagine the scenes as I describe what it might be like to be led into the presence of God. Imagine first that you are standing in a wide-open field—nothing around you but tall grass and blue sky. *(Pause.)* Suddenly, from out of the blue, you hear a voice thunder from heaven. "Look up!" it commands. You raise your head and see a door in the sky; a door standing open to heaven. Beside the door is an angel clothed in white, light streaming all around. *(Pause.)* Then, as the angel reaches out his hand, you hear the same booming voice command, "Come up here, and I will show you the glory of God!"

You take the angel's hand, and immediately find yourself standing in front of an immense throne, towering like a mountain before you. *(Pause.)* Bolts of lightning flash from the base of the throne. Thunder shakes the ground below your feet. You are completely surrounded by the sights and sounds of a cosmic thunderstorm. *(Pause.)* Slowly you realize that you're not alone. Looking first to the left *(pause)*, then to the right *(pause)*, then behind, you see thousands upon thousands of angels stretching as far as your eyes can see. *(Pause.)* Suddenly, without warning, the cracks of lightning and the peals of thunder are overwhelmed by the roar of this heavenly host. "Holy, holy, holy is the Lord God Almighty," they cry. "Holy, holy, holy is the Lord God Almighty. Holy, holy, holy is the Lord God Almighty. To him who sits on the throne be praise and honor and glory and power for ever and ever. Amen."

You stand there, wondering before the God

Then—absolute silence. *(Pause.)* You stand there before the throne, wondering what will happen next. Each second feels like an eternity, but still, only silence *(pause)* until you hear that same thunderous voice coming from the top of throne, commanding you, "Look at me!"

What do you do? Look up? Fall on your face? Look away? Try to hide? Run away? *(Pause.)* What are you feeling right now, knowing that you are standing in the presence of the God of all creation? *(Pause.)* Slowly, finally you raise your head and look at the one who sits on the throne. *(Pause.)* It is the most awe-inspiring and yet comforting sight you could possibly imagine. You are in the very presence of the Lord God Almighty. *(Pause.)*

God has given only a few individuals a glimpse or a vision of his heavenly glory. But God invites each one of us to enter into his presence through worship. *(Pause.)* When we worship God, we need to remember that we are not simply singing songs or repeating words. Rather, we are standing in the actual presence of the God of the entire universe.

we are standing in the actual presence of the God of the entire universe

The Lord of All Creation

Worship Themes:
God is ruler over all.
God created all that exists.

Worship Scriptures:
Genesis 1; 28:12-15; Exodus 13:21-22; John 11:38-44; and Acts 2:2-8

Worship Overview:
Christians often worship God for his love, his holiness, and his help in troubled times. In our busy lives, though, we may be tempted to overlook God's original and most basic revelation of himself—the world he has created. Nature is a reflection of the awesome creativity of God and a demonstration of his power and authority.

This service will help your kids think about how incredibly creative and powerful God must be to create the kind of world we live in. They will also have an opportunity to declare their gratitude for the ways God shows his absolute power in their lives. Use the worship experiences in this service to help your kids take notice of the miracle of God's creation, then take time to celebrate God as ruler of everything they see.

Supply Checklist

- copies of the words to three verses of the song "How Great Thou Art"

- a sheet or a large piece of cloth

- photocopies of the "Powerful Creator" handout (pp. 19-20)

- photocopies of the "God's Amazing Creation" handout (p. 21)
- plenty of art supplies, such as a variety of fabric scraps, fabric paint, permanent markers, stencils, scissors (be sure they can cut fabric), rulers, glitter, and glue

Worship Preparation:
Before the service, find an outdoor natural setting where you can hold this worship service, such as a park, the woods, the mountains, or a lake. Try to find a place that is as secluded and as natural as possible. Arrange transportation for your students, or ask students to meet you there.

Find a place to hang the banner students will make in this worship experience (such as the worship center in your church, a fellowship hall, or your youth room).

Worship Service
Celebration in Song
Praise the Powerful Creator
(5 minutes)

Take your students to a natural setting—such as a park, the woods, the mountains, or a lake—or simply have your students meet there. When everyone has arrived, start the worship service by singing several songs a cappella. You may want to sing songs that focus on God's power and creation, such as the following songs.
- "Awesome God"
- "Crown Him With Many Crowns"
- "I Believe"
- "Lord, I Lift Your Name on High"

During the singing time, encourage kids to celebrate and enjoy the natural surroundings.

Scriptural Celebration
Proclaim God's Power
(10 minutes)

Say: **During this next worship experience, focus on the beautiful evidence of God's creation around us, and the power God demonstrates by holding everything together.**

Give each student a photocopy of the "Powerful Creator" handout (pp. 19-20), and provide lyrics to three verses of "How Great Thou Art." Assign individual students or groups of students to specific portions of the reading assignments on the "Powerful Creator" handout.

Lead kids in singing a verse of "How Great Thou Art," then instruct them to read aloud their assigned parts of the paraphrase of Genesis 1. Then sing another verse of the song, and instruct kids to read their assigned parts of the paraphrases of Exodus 13:21-22; John 11:38-44; Genesis 28:12-15; and Acts 2:2-8. Then lead kids in singing the final verse of "How Great Thou Art."

Personal Reflection
Everything From Nothing
(5 minutes)

Encourage each person to find his or her own quiet spot within the general area. Instruct kids to close their eyes. Say: **I'm going to read aloud a description of what "nothingness" might be like. As I do so, use your imagination to try to understand as best you can the state of nothingness that existed before God created the world.**

Read aloud part 1 of the "God's Amazing Creation" handout (p. 21), and encourage kids to be silent, to keep their eyes closed, and to try to imagine with you what it would be like if the universe did not exist. After you read part 1, have kids open their eyes and read part 2 of the handout.

After you've read the handout, say: **It's impossible for us to completely understand the power and incredible creativity of God in the creation process, partly because we can't comprehend what it means to experience nothingness. God created *everything* out of *nothing*. Everything we see around us sprung from the amazing imagination of God. How wonderful that God chose to use his power to create and sustain such a marvelous place for us to live!**

Leader Tip

Try to read the two parts of the "God's Amazing Creation" handout with expression, enthusiasm, and inspiration. Your vocal expression will affect students' ability to focus on the awe and majesty of God.

Symbolic Displays

Natural Revelation

(10 minutes)

Point to the nature around you and say: **Spend a few minutes looking around for an interesting object that God has created. As you look, think about how that created object reflects God's sustaining power. We'll meet back here with our objects and talk about what we find.**

When students have returned with their objects, have kids form a circle and place their objects in front of them. Encourage each student to display his or her object and answer the following questions:

● **How does your view of God change when you think about God creating this object out of nothing?**
● **How is God's creative process different from our own?**
● **How might this knowledge change your relationship with God?**
● **How is your object a symbol of God's power or authority over creation?**

Encourage students to hang on to their objects for later.

Leader Tip

Check your local park regulations to see if they prohibit the removal of any natural objects. If they do, you can modify this section by gathering objects from your church grounds or your own backyard. Bring them in a box and let your students select an object for this exercise.

Spontaneous Declaration

God's Power in Our Lives

(10 minutes)

Have kids remain in a circle, and encourage them to give spontaneous declarations to God, describing ways God has displayed his power and authority in their lives. Then, after each declaration, instruct the entire group to say aloud in unison: "God is ruler over all. He created everything that exists."

Say: **We'll take turns calling out ways God has shown his power and authority in our lives. When it's your turn, call out a description such as "God, you healed my mother from cancer," "Almighty God, you rescued me from danger last summer at the lake," or "Powerful Creator, your power showed me how to have a relationship with you." After each declaration, we'll say in unison, "God is ruler over all. He created everything that exists." Then the next person can call out another declaration. As you**

Leader Tip

As students search for and collect their symbolic objects, remind them to avoid destroying aspects of nature such as plants, flowers, or bird nests. You might also remind students to stay on established trails if necessary.

participate in this experience, focus on talking directly to God, acknowledging the ways he has shown his power in your life. We'll go around the circle once, then everyone can call out more declarations spontaneously.

When everyone has finished calling out declarations of God's power, pray aloud, thanking God for using his power in the lives of people.

Leader Tip

Depending on the weather and your group's comfort level, you might choose to return to the church for the rest of this worship service.

Symbolic Creation

Reflecting God's Glory

(20 minutes)

Set out a sheet or a large piece of cloth and plenty of art supplies such as a variety of fabric scraps, fabric paint, permanent markers, stencils, scissors (be sure they can cut fabric), rulers, glitter, and glue. Instruct students to work together to create a large banner to represent God's power over creation and in the lives of people. Encourage them to use the art supplies you've provided and, if they want to, to use the natural objects they collected earlier.

When the banner is finished, ask:

● **How is your creative process different from God's creative process?**
● **How is your creative process a reflection of God's?**
● **What can this experience teach you about God's power?**
● **How can thinking about God's power affect the way you use the gifts he has given you?**

Instruct kids to return to your church (or wherever you have decided to hang the banner). When everyone has arrived, have students gather in the place where you've arranged to hang their banner. Instruct kids to work together to hang the banner.

When kids have hung the banner, have them hold hands and form a semicircle around the banner. Encourage kids to name some ways the banner can act as a reminder of God's power and creation. Then allow an open prayer of dedication, asking God to bless their efforts to remind others of God's power in creation and in the lives of people.

The Powerful Creator

Paraphrase of Genesis 1

When God began creating, the earth was shapeless and chaotic. The Spirit of God was hovering over the surface of the water on earth. Then God made the light visible. And God was very happy with the way it looked, and he divided daytime from nighttime. God created the sky to separate the water in the atmosphere from the water on the earth.

Then God separated the water on earth from the dry land, creating the seas. Then God commanded the land to produce all kinds of plants and trees. God set the sun and the moon and the stars in the sky, and they marked the days and the seasons, the months and the years. Then God created great varieties of water animals and birds, and he gave them his blessing. He commanded the animals to reproduce and to fill the waters and the skies with creatures. God then filled the land with land animals of every kind.

Then God created his masterpiece. He fashioned a man from the dirt on the ground. Then he created a companion for the man, the first woman. He gave this man and this woman many characteristics to reflect himself, and he commanded them to reproduce and to fill the earth with humans. He gave them responsibility to care for what he had created. And God was thrilled with what he had made.

Paraphrase of Exodus 13:21-22

In the daytime, God went ahead of the Israelites to show them their way. He showed himself as a huge cloud. In the nighttime, he went ahead of them in the form of a pillar of fire. The fire lit their way at night so they could keep traveling. Every day and every night, God's presence was with the Israelites, and they could see the cloud and the fire in front of them. *(Pause.)*

Paraphrase of John 11:38-44

Jesus went to the tomb where Lazarus was buried. He told the people with him to remove the stone covering the entrance to the tomb. Martha, Lazarus' sister, reminded Jesus that since Lazarus had been dead four days, the odor in the tomb would be strong. Jesus told her she would see the glory of God, and they moved the stone. Then Jesus prayed, asking God the Father to show his glory. Then Jesus said, "Lazarus, come out!" Lazarus walked out of the tomb, still wrapped in linen cloth. *(Pause.)*

The Powerful Creator continued

Paraphrase of Genesis 28:12-15

While Jacob was sleeping, he had a dream. He saw a stairway reaching from earth to heaven, and there were angels going up and down the stairway. God stood in heaven and said, "I am the Lord, the God of your father Abraham and of Isaac. I will give you and your descendants the land you are laying on. God will bless all people on earth through you and your descendants. I am with you, and I will watch over you everywhere you go. Someday I will bring you back to this land. I promise." *(Pause.)*

Paraphrase of Acts 2:2-8

All of a sudden, a loud noise filled the house where the disciples were sitting. Objects that looked like tongues of fire settled on them, and all of the disciples were filled with the Holy Spirit. Through the power of the Holy Spirit, they began to speak in other languages. At that time, there were many Jews who believed in God staying in Jerusalem, where the disciples were. These Jewish people were from all over the world. When they heard the disciples speaking in other languages, the people crowded around in amazement. They heard the disciples speaking in their own languages. They asked, "Aren't these men from Galilee? Why are they speaking our native languages?"

God's Amazing Creation

Read aloud each of the descriptions below.

Part 1

Try to imagine with me a state of nothingness. There are no trees, no grass, no flowers, no people, and no animals. There is no land and no water. There is no such thing as shape or even space. Nothing exists. No color, no shape, no sound, no elements, no vapor, no light, no darkness, no movement, no time. Nothing. *(Pause.)*

Suddenly, out of nothing, God begins to form a world. He brings into being time, space, shape, color, movement, sound, and substance. Suddenly the universe is brought into existence. God creates mass and fills it with elements. The atmosphere takes form. Planets are shaped. The earth becomes a place to sustain life. And then God creates life. The plants begin to grow. The waters explode with life. The earth is crawling with animals. There is color, movement, sound, shape, and life everywhere. And the nothingness has been transformed into everything we can imagine.

Part 2

God's handiwork is displayed all around us. Who else could invent the colors of the rainbow, fill the world with every shape imaginable, cover the earth with beautiful plants, and overwhelm our ears with the sounds of nature? Who else could imagine the ear itself? the eye, the hand, and the heart? Everything God has made shows us his power and his incredible creativity. What a shame that we take it for granted. Stop and look around you. Try to notice God's hand in your surroundings. Remind yourself of the nothingness that existed before. What a powerful and amazing Creator God is!

The Sovereign Lord who Came to Serve

Worship Themes:
God is sovereign.
God became human to serve and save us.

Worship Scriptures:
John 1:1-14; 3:16-17; 13:1-17; Romans 5:6-8; Philippians 2:5-11; and Revelation 1:12-18

Worship Overview:
The Bible tells a beautiful, true story—about a King who laid aside his robes and crown to trade places with the worst criminal in the kingdom—and chose to die in his place, so the criminal could live. It is a story that can be described as an insane rescue, or a reckless act of love, in which the sovereign Son of God deliberately set aside his divine right so he could do for us what we cannot do for ourselves.

Jesus is sovereign God; yet he came to serve (see Matthew 20:25-28). This service will help your kids discover the importance of worship "service" in their own lives, as they experience serving and being served just as Jesus did. Use the worship experiences that follow to help your young people realize that if Jesus "did not come to be served, but to serve," then they too can worship God by serving others.

Supply Checklist

- Bibles
- bowl large enough to wash feet
- towel

- paper and pencils

- words and music to worship songs
- water pitcher
- "servant" items such as a shepherd's crook; stethoscope; new toilet bowl brush; or pictures of a nurse, firefighter, or shepherd

Worship Preparation:
Before the service, select several worship or praise songs to sing.

Place the bowl, water pitcher, and a towel on a small table in front of the group. Put the other symbols here and there around the worship space. Pre-select an outgoing student to read aloud John 1:1-14.

Practice "The Boy and the Butterflies" (pp. 28-29) until you can tell it easily. Or if you prefer, ask one of your dramatically-inclined students to record the story on tape for you.

Worship Service

Opening Celebration

God Is Sovereign

(10 minutes)

Begin by leading several praise and worship songs that emphasize the sovereignty of God. Encourage full participation with such songs as these.

- "Awesome God"
- "Thou Art Worthy"
- "Emmanuel"
- "I Will Sing Unto the Lord"

After five minutes of singing, have your reader read aloud John 1:1-14. Then hand out paper and pencils, and say: **John began his Gospel with the words you have just heard. From these fourteen verses, we can learn a great deal about Jesus, whom John calls the "Word." Please draw a line down the center of your paper. Label the left half "Uncreated things." Label the right half "Created things." Write the name "God" in the appropriate half. Do the same with "animals," "people," "stars," and "plants."** *(Pause.)* **Now listen as** (reader's name) **rereads John 1:1-3. Then, remembering that the Word is Jesus, write "Jesus" in the appropriate half.**

Pause, then ask:

- **Where did you put Jesus? Why?**

Say: **Jesus belongs on the left, in the half that only contains God. Jesus is God, the one who made everything in the universe. And this same Jesus became one of us to do for us something we cannot do for ourselves. The sovereign, all-powerful creator of the universe came into human history to die on the cross for our sins. I want to tell you a story that can help us better understand this incredible teaching of the Bible.**

Worshipful Reflection

God Comes as a Servant

(15 minutes)

Read aloud (or play your recording of) "The Boy and the Butterflies" story (pp. 28-29). When the story ends, say: **Our sovereign God did what the boy in our story could not. God the Son became a human being—Jesus of Nazareth. He gathered followers and showed his love to them by serving them before giving his life for our sins on a rough, wooden cross.**

Form groups of three or four, and give each group a Bible. Assign one of the following questions and verses to each group. Ask groups to first discuss the question, then read the passage to see how it might influence their opinions:

- **What do you think it is like to be Jesus Christ?** (Revelation 1:12-18)
- **Why do you think Jesus became one of us?** (Philippians 2:5-11)
- **Would you have done what Jesus did?** (Romans 5:6-8)

Ask for several volunteers to report their group's responses. Then say: **We certainly don't deserve that kind of love. But God *does* love us—more than life itself. How many of you can recite John 3:16 with me? "For God so loved the world that he gave his one and only Son, that whoever believes in him shall not perish but have eternal life." God loves us because God is love. Jesus demonstrated that love by dying so that we might live forever with him.**

Allow time for students to pray silently to God, thanking him for laying aside his sovereign power to serve us. After a minute of silent prayer, ask a volunteer to close the prayer time by praying something like: **Dear Jesus, even though you are God, you became human in order to die for my sins. Help me to be grateful to you and show that gratitude each day of my life. To you I pray, amen.**

"Jesus called them together and said, 'You know that the rulers of the Gentiles lord it over them, and their high officials exercise authority over them. NOT SO WITH YOU. Instead, whoever wants to become great among you must be your servant, and whoever wants to be first must be your slave—just as the Son of Man did not come to be served, but to serve, and to give his life as a ransom for many.' "

—MATTHEW 20:25-28

FOOT WASHING WORSHIP

The re-enactment of Jesus washing his disciples' feet can be done in a variety of ways. Choose one of the following ideas, or combine the ideas to make one of your own. Then do it with your kids.

● Have different leaders among your group take turns washing each other's feet, and then have them wash the feet of the rest of the group.

● If your group is smaller, you may choose to wash each person's feet yourself.

● If your group is especially large, have everyone remove their shoes and socks while you and a fellow leader prepare the basin and towel. Then, without speaking, go around the room and wash the feet of five or six individuals at random. Although not everyone will have their feet washed, all the kids will feel like a part of the experience because they won't know whose feet you'll choose to wash next.

● If for some reason it isn't feasible for you to wash feet, hands may be substituted. Distribute some newspapers, and have the kids "dirty" their hands with the old ink. Then supply soapy water and a towel so kids can take turns washing each other's hands.

Symbolic Worship

Foot Washing

(20 minutes)

Say: **Jesus demonstrated God's love in a unique way to his disciples just before he died. He washed their feet! By serving his disciples in this humble way, Jesus showed us the way he wants Christians to treat each other—by serving each other.**

One of Jesus' disciples, Peter, was not willing at first to go along with this. You, too, might be uncomfortable. But when we allow our feet to be washed by another, we have a chance to experience God's love in a real, personal way.

Have a volunteer read aloud John 13:1-17 while you silently perform one of the options in the "Foot Washing Worship" box (p. 25). When you are finished, go on to the next part of the service.

Declarative Worship

Worshiping God by Serving Others

(15 minutes)

Say: **After Jesus washed his disciples' feet, he told his disciples that they should follow his example in the way they treat each other. After all, if their Lord and Master was not "above" washing their feet, they, too, shouldn't worry about who was most important, and simply learn to serve each other.**

These days, we also often worry too much about who likes us and how important we are in the group.

Ask:

● **What can we learn from Jesus' lesson?**

● **How has Jesus served you? your family and friends?**

● **Why should we be thankful for the way Jesus has served us?**

Have kids form pairs. Then have partners discuss these questions:

● **How can we express our gratitude to God for serving us?**

● **What are some practical ways we can serve each other in everyday life?**

Ask pairs to plan a pantomime of practical ways they can show thanks to God by serving others. For example, one pair might act out a person picking up trash or playing with younger children.

After three minutes, have kids form a circle. Have each pair act out their act of service and make this statement preceding their presentation: **Because Jesus, our sovereign God, was born to serve me, I can gratefully** (perform your pantomime for the group). For example, you might state, "Because Jesus, our sovereign God, was born to serve me, I can gratefully," then act out a teacher teaching a child about God.

When all the pairs have presented their pantomimes, have kids each join with a new partner, then say: **During our worship service, we have been reminded** of how Jesus our sovereign God came to serve us. And we have discovered many ways we can show our gratitude to God and worship him by serving others. Now you can make this worship experience complete by committing to follow through with your service idea, or another one like it, in the coming week.

Have group members tell their partners what service ideas they'll do in the coming week. The idea can be the one each person acted out or another one like it. Then have pairs close in prayer, thanking God for his sovereignty and service to us, and committing themselves to keeping their promises.

The Boy and THE BUTTERFLIES

Either read or retell in your own words the following story.

There was once a boy who lived in a beautiful, large house where there was a different room to play in for each day of the week. Of all the rooms, however, no room pleased the boy more than the den, where there was a large fireplace; soft, comfortable furniture; and a sliding glass door onto a beautiful garden with a bubbling fountain in the middle. All around the edges of the garden, the gardener had planted the sorts of trees that are particularly loved by Monarch butterflies. Then he had obtained a thousand Monarch caterpillars and turned them loose among the trees.

Sure enough, the caterpillars loved the leaves of the trees, grew strong and fat, spun their cocoons, and hatched out as hundreds and hundreds of beautiful Monarch butterflies. The boy used to spend hours in the garden, watching the beautiful wings of the butterflies catch the light as they flitted to and fro among the trees they loved. Some of the butterflies even lighted on his arms and head when he sat perfectly still for a long time. But then the days began to shorten, and at some signal that only the Monarchs could hear, they flew away, first a few, then the many, and finally even the stragglers.

All winter long, whenever he went into the den, the boy looked out the sliding glass door, pretending that he could see the Monarchs outside, remembering their beauty, and wondering when—or if—they would return.

One day in early spring, well before he had any reason to expect them, the boy noticed what he had been waiting for all winter long. His Monarchs had begun to return. He threw open the sliding glass door and danced out into the garden, scattering the butterflies, who soon returned to the branches where they had been born, and where they would now lay eggs to begin the life cycle all over again. The boy was so happy to see that his dream had come true: His Monarchs had returned home!

A few days later, though, he was horrified! Old Man Winter was not completely banished from the neighborhood, and the thermometer had dropped well below freezing. Soon snow was falling from the sky, freezing snow and sleet, and through the steamed-up window he could see his Monarchs lying in drifts like brown, autumn-colored leaves.

Forgetting his own comfort, the boy threw open the sliding glass door, ran out into the swirling snow, and tried to shoo the butterflies into the safety of the fire-warmed den. Nothing doing. The more he waved at them, the more they fluttered away in the snow. They didn't understand that he was trying to help them.

"What shall I do?" the boy asked himself frantically. "If only I could become one of them. Then I could save them from the cold. I could lead them to safety; I could tell them how to save themselves."

But the boy couldn't become a butterfly. He was as stuck being a human as they were helpless butterflies in the storm.

This story does not have a happy ending. As such, it is very different from the story it is meant to illustrate. For unlike the poor little rich boy of the story, when the Son of God looked down from heaven upon the perilous plight of humankind, there was something he could do. In the mysterious majesty of God's infinite power and unbelievable love, Jesus was born in Bethlehem, "not . . . to be served, but to serve, and to give his life as a ransom for many." He became one of us not merely to show us the way, but to be our Way in from the cold of separation and despair to the warmth and joy of life with God.

The butterflies of our story all died, but that need not be so with us. When we accept Jesus as our Lord and Savior, God promises us joy and happiness with him forever.

("The Boy and the Butterflies" story is loosely based on a story "The Man and the Birds" told by radio personality Paul Harvey. For more information, contact Paul Harvey News at (312) 899-4085.)

The Lord who Is Holy

Worship Themes:

God is holy.
God forgives our sins.

Worship Scriptures:

Psalms 130; 131; Isaiah 6:1-7; Mark 14:66-72; 15:33-41; and Romans 8:1-9

Worship Overview:

Christians enjoy singing the praises of God. We sing, "Our God is an awesome God" and "Holy, Holy, Holy," but we don't often reflect on the deep meaning of the words we sing. "Holiness" is not a concept or term used often by teenagers today. Yet it is central to understanding God. Only when we begin to sense the true holiness of God can we become more aware of how deeply our sin disappoints God. And only when we see the depth of God's disappointment can we begin to understand how incredible it is that our Holy God is willing to forgive us.

In this worship experience, you can help your kids develop a better understanding of God's holy nature and their own sin. And through confession, they'll experience God's forgiveness and understand the joy of being restored to a close relationship with God.

Use this service to lead students to be recommitted to following God through worship in their daily lives.

Supply Checklist

- Bibles
- a table lamp
- black construction paper
- CD or tape player with soft meditative music
- masking tape
- paper
- pens or pencils
- a cross, two- to three-feet tall
- index cards

Worship Preparation:

Before the service, set up a "worship center" table at the front of the meeting room. On the table, set the lamp and cross. Use a cross from your church, or you may make a rough cross out of branches and twine. Since the cross will need to stand upright, you can place the base of the branch cross in a can of sand.

Write each of the following on a separate index card: GOD, SIN, HOLY, ISAIAH, PETER, ME. Set up the CD or cassette player and music so it's ready for use when needed in the worship service. Have the rest of the supplies available for use when needed.

Select the songs to be sung at the opening and closing.

Worship Service

Declarative Celebration

Worship God's Holiness

(10 minutes)

Begin the worship experience by leading the group in several songs that stress the holiness, majesty, and glory of God. Sing songs such as the following.

- "Awesome God"
- "Glorify Thy Name"
- "He Is Exalted"
- "I Exalt Thee"
- "Seek Ye First"

After five minutes of singing, say: **Now let's create our own "Declaration of Worship" to God. I will say the words, "Our God is..." then you will take turns completing the sentence with a word or a phrase. Examples might be awesome, worthy of praise, creator, or powerful. After each response, we'll all clap our hands one time. Clapping in American Sign Language means "praise." In Psalm 98:8 clapping is referred to as one way creation praises God. So our hand clap will be an act of praise following each of our declarations.**

Have kids form a circle, then choose a volunteer to begin the Declaration of Worship. Each time you say, "Our God is..." allow a different person to declare a truth about God, then have the class clap their hands once in unison. Continue until everyone has made a declaration about God.

Scriptural Reflection

Sin and Holiness

(10 minutes)

Ask one of the participants to read Isaiah 6:1-3 to the group. Then have kids form pairs, and distribute a sheet of paper and a pen or pencil to each pair. On the paper, ask pairs to write the words "God is" horizontally and then the word "holy" vertically.

Around the "word cross," ask pairs to write words or phrases beginning with the letters of "holy" that help us understand God's holiness. Some examples are hallowed, honored, high, overall, omnipotent, opening doors for us, loving, Lord of all, lasting, your best friend, your Savior. After one minute, ask volunteers to share some of their words. Then have partners discuss these questions:

- **Do you understand God's holiness? Why or why not?**
- **Why is it hard for us to understand God's holiness?**

After the discussion, tape the "GOD" card on the wall at about eye level. Then show students the "HOLY" card and ask:

- **Where should we place this card to show how close holiness is to God?**

Tape it next to the "GOD" card as kids indicate. Now show them the "SIN" card and ask:

● **Where should we place this card to show how close sin is to God?**

Tape it on the wall as kids indicate. Read aloud Isaiah 6:4-5, then show students the "ISAIAH" card and ask:

● **Where should this card be placed to represent the distance Isaiah felt from God?**

Place his card near the "SIN" card and say: **We see that we are separated from our holy God by our sin.**

"In the year that King Uzziah died, I saw the Lord seated on a throne, high and exalted, and the train of his robe filled the temple. Above him were seraphs, each with six wings: With two wings they covered their faces, with two they covered their feet, and with two they were flying. And they were calling to one another: *'Holy, holy, holy is the Lord Almighty; the whole earth is full of his glory.' "—Isaiah 6:1-3*

Symbolic Reflection

Sin and Forgiveness

(25 minutes)

Turn on the lamp. Invite students to get comfortable, then have them close their eyes, and turn off the rest of the lights in the room—but not the lamp. Give kids each paper and a pencil.

Read aloud Mark 14:66-72. Then have kids think quietly about this question: **How do you think God felt when Peter denied knowing his son, Jesus?** While kids are thinking, tape the "PETER" card next to the "SIN" and "ISAIAH" cards.

Then say: **We all have times in our lives when we don't act like children of God. For example, when we put other people down, when we gossip, when we hate, when we cheat, when we misuse the Lord's name, when we take advantage of others. Reflect quietly on times in your own life when you have not acted like a child of God.** *(Pause.)* **How do you think God felt at those times?** *(Pause.)* **On your paper, write words or draw symbols to illustrate one of the times you did not act like a child of God. These will not be shared with anyone.**

After thirty seconds, show kids the "ME" card. Tape it next to the cards that say "SIN," "ISAIAH," and "PETER." Say: **We, too, are separated from God by our sin. When we are separated from God, we are often also separated from other people. For example, whenever there is gossip, prejudice, put-downs, swearing, or uncontrolled anger, we find we are separated from God and each other. In those times, we are a great distance from being like God—being holy.**

On the other side of your paper, write "Holy" in the middle of the sheet and draw a small circle around the word. Next draw four additional concentric circles, each larger than the last, until the largest covers most of the page.

If necessary, show students an example of what you want them to draw.

Say: **Reflect on your life the last forty-eight hours. Remember as many events as possible. As you remember each event, draw a star to represent the experience on your diagram. If you felt "holy" or close to God in the experience, draw your star close to the center small circle. If the experience made you feel "sinful" or separated from God, draw your star in the outermost circle. If the experience had no impact on your relationship with God, draw your star between the inner and outer circles. This diagram will not be shared with anyone else.**

Allow two minutes for students to create their diagrams. Then have kids reflect silently on these questions:

- **Where are most of the stars on your diagram?**
- **What does your diagram tell you about your relationship with God?**
- **What does your diagram tell you about your sin? your indifference?**
- **How do you think your diagram makes God feel?**

Give each person a sheet of black construction paper and a strip of tape. Say: **While soft music is played, I invite you to tape your black paper onto the** cross at the front of the room. **This act symbolizes how our sins—including the sin of indifference—separate our lives from God's holiness. As the symbols of our sins cover the cross, we, like Peter, have denied God and his Son.** Play soft music as the students tape their black papers onto the cross. When everyone is finished, read Mark 15:33-41. Then turn off the lamp, and say: **Our sin brings darkness and dims God's light in the world.**

Turn on the lamp again, and read aloud Psalm 130 to the group. After the reading, form groups of five or fewer, and give each group paper and pencils. In the groups ask one person to read Psalm 131 and one to read Romans 8:1-9. After the readings, say: **Each group now has two minutes to write a one-sentence sermon on the theme of forgiveness based on the Scriptures we just read.**

After two minutes, invite each group to share its sentence sermons. As groups share, slowly remove the black sheets of paper from the cross. After the last sheet of paper is removed, point to the cross and ask:

● **How does it feel to be forgiven?**

Say: **God's forgiveness gives us a great reason to worship his holiness. And we can worship his holiness not only through worship experiences like this one but also through the way we live every day.**

Personal Reflection

Called to Holiness

(5 minutes)

Have students turn to Isaiah 6:1-7. Say: **We read the first three verses earlier. Now I will read verses 1 through 7. This tells us about Isaiah's sin and God's forgiveness.** Read the passage to the group. Then give each person another sheet of paper. Say: **On this paper, write a prayer to God that expresses your feelings about his forgiveness in your life.** Tell kids their prayers can be as short as one sentence or as long as a page.

When kids finish, ask them to turn their papers over and write one way they'll worship God from now on by pursuing holiness in their lives. For example, kids might write, "I will stop drinking," "I will abstain from sex until I am married," or "I will spend consistent time with God every day." Play soft music while kids write out their commitments.

After a minute, say: **Fold your paper so no one can see what you've written. During this time of commitment, I invite you to bring your prayer and commitment and lay it at the foot of the cross. This symbolizes your agreement with God to thank and praise him and to follow him in your life. This act is done in front of others as a public symbol of your renewed commitment to follow Jesus.** Once again play soft music as students place their commitments at the cross.

Leader Tip

Hymns you may want to sing during the closing might include: "Redeemed"; "Savior, Like a Shepherd Lead Us"; "Lead On, O King Eternal"; and "Crown Him With Many Crowns."

Closing Celebration

Committed to Follow

(5 minutes)

To close the worship experience, lead the group in singing songs that will help solidify their commitment, such as the following.

- "Find Us Faithful"
- "I'm Yours"
- "I Believe"
- "I Will Call Upon the Lord"

After five minutes, lead kids in prayer, praising God for his holiness and thanking him for his forgiveness in our lives.

The Lord Who Defeated Death

Worship Themes:

God is all-powerful.
God defeated death for us.

Worship Scriptures:

Psalms 23; 93; and Matthew 26:17–28:20

Worship Overview:

Jesus Christ's final week on earth was undoubtedly agonizing for him. He was ridiculed, humiliated, spat upon, unjustly convicted, and killed. His death was brutal. Some taunted Jesus by asking why his God did not rescue him from the agony. Others, who claimed to love him, abandoned him when he needed them most. Yet we know the outcome of Christ's pain was a glorious resurrection—establishing Jesus as the all-powerful Lord and King of all creation.

This worship experience will enable your students to dramatize the events of Jesus' last week—including his death and resurrection. As they step back in time, they, too, may be able to experience some of the painful realities that Jesus faced. And as they portray his death and resurrection, they, too, can praise our all-powerful God for defeating death for us.

Use the worship experiences that follow to help students discover how God defeated death for them—through Jesus' death and resurrection.

Supply Checklist

- Bibles
- a table covered with a colored cloth

- props for the drama of the Lord's Supper—cups, juice, and bread
- masking tape
- markers
- CD or cassette player with CDs or cassettes of Christian music
- food for the love feast—olives, grapes, prunes, dates, cheeses, bread, crackers, and fruit juices

- costume material to be used in the drama (optional)
- napkins

- newsprint

Worship Preparation:

Place the table against a wall, and place the food for the love feast on the table.

Place the props for the drama at one end of the room. Have the other supplies available for use when needed. Select the songs to be sung at the opening and closing of the worship experience.

Worship Service

Group Worship Preparation

Preparing to Worship
(15 minutes)

Leader Tip

If your group is small, you can combine the Scriptures so groups have more than one Scripture to act out. Or simply read the unassigned Scripture portions between dramas as a bridge from one presentation to the next.

Have music playing softly as students arrive, and invite them to be seated. When everyone has arrived, say: **This worship experience will involve each of us in some unique ways. Before we can begin the worship service, we need to do some preparation. The first thing we need to do is form groups of three or four. Each group will be assigned a Scripture passage that describes some scene from Jesus' last days on earth. Your assignment is to work with your group to develop a skit telling the story of what happened in your assigned Scripture. Some props are available, but you can use anything in the room that you think will work. You have ten minutes to read the Scripture you're assigned and develop your skit, which will be presented to the entire group during the worship experience.**

Now assign the Scriptures listed to the groups. Encourage them to begin by asking one group member to read the Scripture and then move as quickly as possible in assigning parts and getting ready for their drama. Make sure all the group members participate in their group's presentation. Here are the Scriptures:

A. The Lord's Supper (Matthew 26:26-30)

B. Jesus Prays (Matthew 26:36-46)

C. Jesus Is Arrested (Matthew 26:47-55)

D. Jesus Before the Council (Matthew 26:57-67)

E. Jesus Before Pilate (Matthew 27:1-2,11-26)

F. Jesus Is Crucified (Matthew 27:32-44)

G. He Is Risen (Matthew 28:1-10)

H. Jesus Before the Disciples (Matthew 28:16-20)

After ten minutes, ask groups to gather together.

Leader Tip

As a variation on this worship experience, you may want groups to prepare their dramas prior to the worship experience. A week or so before the worship service, ask specific groups of kids to work together to prepare a drama of one or more of your assigned Scripture passages. Then have groups come to the worship service ready to present their dramas.

Symbolic Celebration

Love Feast
(10 minutes)

Say: **Listen as I read Matthew 26:17-20.**

Read the passage, then say: **I invite you to come to the table and eat. Jesus loved his disciples, and Jesus loves us. Come and eat. While the** music plays and you're enjoying the food, find at least two other people and pray together, thanking Jesus for bringing us life and nourishment, and saving us from death. When the music fades, please take a seat once again. The love feast will last about five minutes.

After five minutes, fade the music out and say: **Now the group that prepared drama A (based on Matthew 26:26-30) will come and present its drama for us. This is what happened at the love feast Jesus ate with his disciples.** Have kids present their drama.

Next, lead the group in one or two songs that reflect the power of God. Here are some suggestions.
- "Awesome God"
- "He Is Exalted"
- "What a Mighty God We Serve"
- "Humble Thyself in the Sight of the Lord"

Worshipful Reflection
The Message of Christ's Death
(15 minutes)

Say: **We will now have the groups who worked on the following dramas present their skits to us:**

B. Jesus Prays (Matthew 26:36-46)

C. Jesus Is Arrested (Matthew 26:47-55)

D. Jesus Before the Council (Matthew 26:57-67)

After the dramas, say: **Reflect silently upon the things Jesus experienced in the Scriptures we've dramatized.** Ask kids to quietly consider their responses to these questions:
- **How would you have felt if you had been in Jesus' place?**
- **What would you have done if you had been a member of the council? Now we will have the two more groups present their skits to us.**

E. Jesus Before Pilate (Matthew 27:1-2,11-26)

F. Jesus Is Crucified (Matthew 27:32-44)

Again ask the students to quietly consider their responses to these questions:
- **What would you have done if you had been Pilate?**
- **What would you have done if you had been a witness to the killing of Jesus?**

After the reflection time, have kids form new groups of three by finding two other people from different drama groups. Have the trios discuss these questions:
- **What signs of God's weakness seem to be present in the Scripture dramas we have just seen?**
- **What signs in our society today seem to indicate that God is dead or at least very weak?**

Allow one minute for groups to discuss each question, then invite groups to share their thoughts with the entire group. Say: **Thank you for sharing. These are not easy things to think about.**

Declarative Praise

The Message of Christ's Victory

(10 minutes)

Say: **Thankfully, Jesus' life did not end on the cross. God was not dead. God was not finished. God had not lost his power! The last two groups will now present their dramas.**

G. He Is Risen (Matthew 28:1-10)

H. Jesus Before the Disciples (Matthew 28:16-20)

After the dramas, have kids return to their trios and discuss these questions:

● **What signs of God's power were present in the Scripture dramas we just saw?**

● **What signs do you see in our society that show God is alive and powerful and strong?**

After a few minutes, have trios share their answers with the entire group.

Give a sheet of newsprint and a marker to each trio. Say: **At the top of your newsprint write, "God, your power is..." Halfway down the sheet write the words, "God, I feel your power when..."**

Once the groups do this, say: **Complete these sentences in as many ways as you can. Remember there are no wrong answers!**

Allow two minutes for kids to work. Have groups tape their newsprint lists to the wall. Then say: **Now we'll use some of your thoughts for a declaration of worship to God. God wants us to speak our beliefs about him. I will say, "God, your power is..." and then I'll wait for a response. Once one person has said a response, we'll all say together, "Oh, yeah, God's power is** (repeat the word or phrase that someone has just shared). **Then once again I'll say, "God, your power is..." Then someone will share, and we will all respond.**

Once students understand, begin the declaration. Continue as long as kids continue to make declarations about God.

Symbolic Celebration

The God Who Defeated Death

(10 minutes)

Say: **Turn to Psalm 93. We will read this responsively—with the guys reading the odd-numbered verses and the gals reading the even-numbered verses. Everyone ready? Guys, let's begin.**

After the psalm, ask:

● **What does this psalm say to you about God's power?**

Say: **Please sit quietly, close your eyes, and listen as I read another Psalm.**

Read aloud Psalm 23. Then say: **Now let us praise God that in his great power he overcame death once and for all. Because of him we have life eternal.** Select and sing one song of faith and victory, such as these.

- "Awesome God"
- "I Believe"
- "What a Mighty God We Serve"
- "As the Deer"
- "Humble Thyself in the Sight of the Lord"

After the song, lead the group in a prayer thanking God for using his great power to defeat death for us.

The Lord Whose Word Is True

Worship Themes:
God is truth.
God gave us his true Word.

Worship Scriptures:
Deuteronomy 18:15; Psalm 68:18; Isaiah 53:3,7,11-12; Matthew 26:62; 27:38; 28:5-10; Luke 23:34; 24:50; John 1:11; 6:14; Acts 1:9-11; 2 Timothy 3:16-17; and Hebrews 13:8

Worship Overview:
In the movie, *The Treasure of the Sierra Madre*, Humphrey Bogart plays the part of a novice prospector who wants to strike it rich. At the end of a long day's trek through brutal mountains, he sits dejectedly, moaning about his bad luck.

That's when an old prospector who'd joined the expedition jumps up and dances a jig. Bogart thinks he's gone crazy, and tells him to celebrate when they find gold.

The old prospector slaps his knee, points to the ground, and laughs. "You don't even know what you're sittin' on!"

Bogart was sitting on a mountain laced with gold. A fortune. He just didn't recognize it.

Many Christian teenagers are in the same position. They're looking for truth. They long for at least one certainty, one bedrock foundation in a shifting world. Someplace solid to build their lives.

And all the while, back home their Bibles gather dust.

During this worship experience, you'll encourage your teenagers to focus on two facts: God is truth, and God has given us his true Word. There *is* a solid foundation for life—and it's the Word of God.

God is worthy of our praise and worship for being who he is: true and unchanging.

Supply Checklist

- Bibles
- a science textbook
- paper towels
- a supermarket tabloid
- tape
- copies of the "Prophecy and Fulfillment" handout (pp. 48-49) tape
- a TV schedule
- a high school yearbook
- a flower
- newsprint
- markers
- a pad of red ink

Worship Preparation:

Before the service, select worship or praise songs to sing during the "Opening Celebration."

Review the "Prophecy and Fulfillment" responsive reading (pp. 48-49) until you're comfortable with it and can read it dramatically.

Tape a large sheet of newsprint to the wall. Place the red ink pad where you can easily retrieve it for the closing worship activity.

Worship Service

Opening Celebration

God and His Word Are True

(10 minutes)

Encourage your teenagers to be involved in leading singing. You'll help develop their leadership skills and heart for service, as well as have time with them during practice sessions. Here are some songs that will help your group focus on the theme.

- "Father, I Adore You"
- "Great Is the Lord"
- "Lord, Be Glorified"
- "Change My Heart, Oh God"
- "God Is So Good"

After about ten minutes, end your time of singing with the song, "God Is So Good."

Declaring the Truth

God Is True

(15 minutes)

Ask: **Where do you go to find truth?**

After a few kids respond, say: **That question has been around for thousands of years. Some people rely on their feelings and experiences, but feelings change—sometimes very quickly—and experiences can be misleading.**

Or is truth made up of those things that can be duplicated in a science lab? verified by witnesses? communicated through aliens?

People look for truth in many places. Let's see which places you think are most reliable. Ask for six volunteers. Give each volunteer one of the following: a supermarket tabloid, a TV schedule, a science textbook, a high school yearbook, and a flower. Give one volunteer nothing at all.

Say: **The question is, "Where do you find truth?" I'll ask our volunteers to hold up their objects one at a time. We'll vote about which sources of truth you think are most reliable. We'll measure your response by how loudly you applaud.**

Volunteer 1, hold up the tabloid, please. Applaud if you turn to tabloids to learn what's true. *(Pause for applause.)*

Volunteer 2, hold up the TV schedule, please. Applaud if you turn to television and other media to learn what's true. *(Pause for applause.)*

Volunteer 3, hold up the science textbook, please. Applaud if you turn to science to learn what's true. *(Pause for applause.)*

Volunteer 4, hold up the yearbook, please. Applaud if you turn to your friends to learn what's true. *(Pause for applause.)*

Volunteer 5, hold up the flower, please. Applaud if you rely on your feelings to know what's true. *(Pause for applause.)*

Volunteer 6, hold up your arm please. You can't see it from where you're sitting, but this volunteer sports a very touching "Mom" tattoo. Applaud if you rely on your parents to learn what's true. *(Pause for applause.)*

Ask:

● **What other sources do you rely on to discover truth?**

List teenagers' suggestions on newsprint. Then ask for applause for each of the additional items. (If nobody suggests the Bible as a source, raise the suggestion yourself.) Based on the applause you heard for all the items, list their top two choices on the newsprint. Then say: **So these are your top choices as sources of truth. Let's give our volunteers a hand!**

Collect items as your volunteers return to their seats. Then say: **But what *is* truth? Let's at least describe it. Call out words that to you describe truth. Some words might be "unchanging" or "sincere." What are others?**

Write suggested words on newsprint. Then say: **Good words! A question for you: Can you think of a Bible passage—or an example in the Bible—of how God is true in these ways? For instance, if on our list we have the word "consistent," I might mention that Jesus is the same yesterday, today, and tomorrow (Hebrews 13:8). Don't worry if you can't quote the verse exactly; a paraphrase in your own words is fine.**

Ask teenagers to form pairs, read through the list, then decide which of the words bring to mind an example of how God reflects that quality. They can quote a verse, paraphrase a verse, or explain an example from the Bible. Give pairs two minutes to come up with an idea, then ask pairs to share their ideas with the whole group.

After your kids affirm ways God is true, say, **We just sang the song, "God Is So Good." Join me in singing the song again, and let's substitute the synonyms and descriptions on our list to complete the verse, "God is so..."**

After teenagers sing a number of the verses that they've created, ask students to form trios and discuss:

● **Why is it important that God is true?**

● **What difference does it make in your life that God is truth?**

Say: **God is truth, and God gave us his true Word. We are witnesses to God's truth. Here are markers—if you've seen God's truth in your life, come forward and write your initials on the newsprint next to the word that describes your experience.**

Worshipful Reflection
God's Word Is True
(15 minutes)

Say: **To tell whether a piece of lumber is true, you can measure it with a measuring tape and see if it is straight by using a square. To tell whether a law is true, you can test it in a courtroom before a judge. But how do you test God to see if he is true? What do you think?**

List kids' responses on newsprint. Then say: **One way to see if God is true, reliable, and trustworthy is to ask: Does God keep his word?**

Before class prepare enough photocopies of the "Prophecy and Fulfillment" responsive reading (pp. 48-49) so there's one for every two students. Have the students form pairs and then divide the pairs into two groups. Distribute the copies of the responsive reading. Assign student A readings to one group and student B readings to the other group. Then read "Prophecy and Fulfillment" responsively.

After the reading, have kids form a circle for the next experience.

Leader Tip

If responsive readings are a new element of worship for your youth group, explain to them that each group reads its part aloud in unison.

"All Scripture is God-breathed and is useful for teaching, rebuking, correcting and training in righteousness, SO THAT THE MAN OF GOD MAY BE THOROUGHLY EQUIPPED FOR EVERY good work."

—2 Timothy 3:16-17

Symbolic Declaration

Covenant of Truth

(10 minutes)

Leader Tip

Have paper towels on hand for teenagers to use to clean their thumbs.

Say: **God has given us his true Word here in the Bible. To know God we must know what he has revealed about himself through the Bible. But so what? What difference does it make in our lives if we know God's Word?**

After several teenagers respond, ask a volunteer to read aloud 2 Timothy 3:16-17. Then say: **The Apostle Paul writes that God's Word is dynamic. Knowing it needs to make a difference. It teaches us. Corrects us. Trains us. The Bible helps us know who God is, what he wants, and what he's doing in the world. So it's important we know and respect it as God's Word.**

When judges are elected, they promise to uphold the law. It's important we agree to live according to the true Word of God here in the Bible. As an act of worship to God, let's agree to become people of the Book—to actively, willingly, joyfully seek to live according to God's true Word. Doing so is our sincerest way of worshiping God.

Hold up a Bible, and say: **If you'll make that commitment along with me, please join me in placing your thumb print in this Bible. In this book we read about many blood sacrifices made by God's people to atone for sin. But the last sacrifice described is the one that was also made for us: Jesus' sacrifice on the cross. As we commit ourselves to being a people of the Book, let's leave our thumb prints in red ink—a grateful reminder of the precious blood that's been shed for us.**

Simply roll your thumb in this ink pad (demonstrate) **and place your thumb print here on this page. We'll let our unique thumb prints represent our decision to live in a way that follows God's Word.**

After all teenagers who wish to participate have done so, join hands in a circle and close with prayer. Thank God for being Truth—and giving us his truth.

Prophecy and Fulfillment

Leader: God is truth and his Word is true. By his own words we will declare him to be trustworthy. His Word was written through many men over thousands of years; his Word stands as a reliable witness. Let's measure God by his own words.

In God's Word he declared that his Son would be a prophet. It is written in Deuteronomy 18:15 that "The Lord your God will raise up for you a prophet like me from among your own brothers. You must listen to him." And in John 6:14 we find the fulfillment of God's Word...

A Students: "After the people saw the miraculous sign that Jesus did, they began to say, 'Surely this is the Prophet who is to come into the world.'"

Leader: But this promised prophet of God would not be accepted by all people. He came to love, but this love triggered hatred in his own people. Isaiah 53:3 records, "He was despised and rejected by men, a man of sorrows, and familiar with suffering. Like one from whom men hide their faces he was despised, and we esteemed him not."

The Apostle John records in John 1:11 that...

B Students: "He came to that which was his own, but his own did not receive him." God's Word is true.

Leader: God knew that Jesus would be rejected and sent him anyway, just as God promised. Even before Jesus was born, God told us Jesus would be arrested and tried. And in his defense he would remain quiet. It is written in Isaiah 53:7 that "He was oppressed and afflicted, yet he did not open his mouth; he was led like a lamb to the slaughter, and as a sheep before her shearers is silent, so he did not open his mouth." God's Word is truth, because it is recorded in Matthew 26:62...

A Students: "Then the high priest stood up and said to Jesus, 'Are you not going to answer? What is this testimony that these men are bringing against you?'"

Leader: "But Jesus remained silent. The high priest said to him, 'I charge you under oath by the living God: Tell us if you are the Christ, the Son of God.'"

B Students: God knew that Jesus would die years before he was born. God also knew that Jesus would be crucified with sinners.

Leader: In God's Word it is recorded in Isaiah 53:12, "Therefore I will give him a portion among the great, and he will divide the spoils with the strong, because he poured out his life unto death, and was numbered with the transgressors. For he bore the sin of many, and made intercession for the transgressors."

A Students: Once again, God has given us his true word. Matthew 27:38 records, "Two robbers were crucified with him, one on his right and one on his left."

Leader: God said Jesus would pray for his enemies. God wrote this in Isaiah 53:12 where it is written, "For he bore the sin of many, and made intercession for the transgressors."

B Students: God is truth and so is his Word. In Luke 23:34 it is recorded, "Jesus said, 'Father, forgive them, for they do not know what they are doing.'" God's Word is true.

Leader: Then God declares the impossible. God states that Jesus would resurrect from the dead. In Isaiah 53:11, it says, "After the suffering of his soul, he will see the light of life and be satisfied."

A Students: And God's Word is true! In Matthew 28:5-10, the historian records…

Leader: "The angel said to the women, 'Do not be afraid, for I know that you are looking for Jesus, who was crucified. He is not here; he has risen, just as he said. Come and see the place where he lay. Then go quickly and tell his disciples: "He has risen from the dead and is going ahead of you into Galilee. There you will see him." Now I have told you.' So the women hurried away from the tomb, afraid yet filled with joy, and ran to tell his disciples. Suddenly Jesus met them. 'Greetings,' he said. They came to him, clasped his feet and worshiped him. Then Jesus said to them, 'Do not be afraid. Go and tell my brothers to go to Galilee; there they will see me.'"

B Students: God's Word said that Jesus would ascend into heaven.

Leader: Psalm 68:18 says, "When you ascended on high, you led captives in your train; you received gifts from men, even from the rebellious—that you, O Lord God, might dwell there."

A Students: And it's true! In Luke 24:50, the writer records, "When he had led them out to the vicinity of Bethany, he lifted up his hands and blessed them. While he was blessing them, he left them and was taken up into heaven."

Leader: It is recorded that Jesus one day will return. Acts 1:9-11 says, "After he said this, he was taken up before their very eyes, and a cloud hid him from their sight. They were looking intently up into the sky as he was going, when suddenly two men dressed in white stood beside them. 'Men of Galilee,' they said, 'why do you stand here looking into the sky? This same Jesus, who has been taken from you into heaven, will come back in the same way you have seen him go into heaven.'"

Jesus has not yet returned. However, because God has always been true to his Word, we look for his return.

B Students: We are sure that God is truth and God gave us his true Word.

Together: God has been true to the Word he has given us. His promises have all come true. Based on this evidence, we declare together in one strong voice, "God is truth, and he has given us his true Word."

The Lord who Draws Close to us

Worship Themes:
God is high above us.
God draws close to us.

Worship Scriptures:
Isaiah 9:6-7; Luke 22:15-20; John 1:1-5, 10-14; Philippians 2:9-11; and Revelation 19:12, 16

Worship Overview:
One thing about the Kingdom of God: There's plenty of room for mystery and paradox. True leaders serve others. You save your life by giving it away. You find real freedom when you become a slave of Christ.

And the most amazing mystery of all: The mighty God who is high above us, whose glory fills every majestic corner of the cosmos, knows and draws close to each of us—*personally*.

In this worship service, you'll help your teenagers grab hold of both ends of this paradox: The God who is high above us has also drawn close to us. And he's been at it since the beginning. From the dawn of creation, God has set his sights on having a loving relationship with your teenagers—not as just creations, but as sons and daughters, adopted into the Kingdom.

Use these worship experiences to invite your teenagers into the mystery of God's loving call to them, and help them respond to it.

Supply Checklist

- Bibles
- modeling clay

- crayons
- pens or pencils
- markers
- tape
- newsprint
- elements of Communion
- CD or cassette player for playing Gregorian chant music (optional)

- a print of Michelangelo's "Creation of Adam" from the Sistine Chapel in art book at local library
- four copies of the "God Draws Close" script (pp. 56-57)

- a manger scene

Worship Preparation:

Before the service, select several worship or praise songs to sing during the celebration time.

Visit your library to obtain a print of Michelangelo's "Creation of Adam." (A photograph of the painting appears in many collections of Michelangelo's work.) Have your example of this art ready to show the group.

If you've decided to have some students create a slide show or video to go along with the readers theater, give those students copies of the "God Draws Close" readers theater script (pp. 56-57) and a list of suggested images for a slide show or video from the Leader Tip on page 55. Be sure to preview their work before the worship service.

worship Service
Reflections on Truth

Awesome Sights

(5 minutes)

In a pair share, ask students to describe the most awesome sight or event they've ever encountered. When they've finished describing it, ask them to sum up their response to the sight or event in two or three words.

When pairs finish, have a few of them call out some of the events that they found awesome and the words that summed up their response to it. Then say: **It's tough to find words to describe an awesome experience. Those sort of situations are often beyond description. The writers of the Bible had the opportunity to see and experience a little of God's awesome glory—and they struggled to sum up in words what they experienced. Consider just these few names of Jesus, drawn from biblical accounts.**

Read the following aloud:

"For to us a child is born, to us a son is given, and the government will be on his shoulders. And he will be called Wonderful Counselor, Mighty God, Everlasting Father, Prince of Peace."

"Therefore God exalted him to the highest place and gave him the name that is above every name, that at the name of Jesus every knee should bow, in heaven and on earth and under the earth, and every tongue confess that Jesus Christ is Lord, to the glory of God the Father."

"His eyes are like blazing fire, and on his head are many crowns. He has a name written on him that no one knows but he himself. On his robe and on his thigh he has this name written: KING OF KINGS AND LORD OF LORDS." (Isaiah 9:6, Philippians 2:9-11; and Revelation 19:12,16)

Say: **No matter how awestruck we were by the experiences we've discussed—God is far more awesome! John's response to God's awesome nature was to worship him—and that can be our response as well. God is high above us and worthy of praise.**

Declaring the Truth

Instant Art
(15 minutes)

Say: **Many of you are familiar with the artist Michelangelo's magnificent painting of the "Creation of Adam" on the vault of the Sistine Chapel at the Vatican in Rome. In Michelangelo's painting, a powerful God, surrounded by cherubs, reaches a mighty fingertip toward Adam, who stretches back toward God—and they almost touch.**

Place the artwork where your group can easily see it. Then say: **Imagine for a moment walking into the Sistine Chapel. The chapel is smaller than you thought it would be, and crowded with visitors. Because the Chapel is considered a place of worship as well as an art treasure, you're asked to stay silent—to simply look—and to let the walls and ceiling of the chapel inspire you. Your eyes rise, looking high above the altar, and then you see it: this massive painting that covers the ceiling. What do you think when you see it? What do you feel? Let's share some of our responses aloud.**

After a few volunteers have shared, say: **We don't know everything Michelangelo thought during the years he lay on his back painting the Sistine Chapel ceiling. But we *do* know that his art beautifully illustrates how far above us God really is. God is a life-giver without whom Adam would never have drawn a breath.**

Form trios, and together choose a scene in the Bible that demonstrates that God is high above us—and that he's powerful and mighty. Examples might include Jesus on the cross, God at Creation, Jesus raising Lazarus, or John seeing a vision of heaven. Decide how you can illustrate that moment without using words. You can create a "freeze," which means you'll get in a position that illustrates the moment you've chosen, and we'll guess what you're doing. Or you can draw a poster, or make a small statue out of modeling clay. In your groups, select a moment to illustrate and a way to do it. Then take five minutes to make your creation. You'll then share your creation with the entire group.

After five minutes, ask groups to take turns presenting their creations. Ask other groups to guess what's being portrayed. As each creation is identified, ask the students who presented it why they chose that scene and why they think it demonstrates God is far above us.

Then ask:
- **What quality of God does your creation depict?**
- **How does this quality place God far above us?**

When all groups have finished, ask teenagers to join you in a circle and to praise God for his qualities that are so far above us.

Leader Tip

To give an added dimension to this readers theater, consider asking several of your teenagers to create a slide show (or video) to accompany the reading. Give them a copy of the activity several weeks before you intend to use this worship service. Encourage their creativity, but be sure they understand this is a serious reading, and preview their work before letting it be shown to the entire group. Some suggested visual ideas are keyed to the numbers in the margin of the reading (see pps. 56 and 57), but encourage teenagers to brainstorm their own approach.

Group Celebration

Celebration of an Awesome God

(10 minutes)

Recruit students to lead singing. Then guide kids to worship God with songs that focus on God's power and might. Here are some possible song choices.

- "Awesome God"
- "Big House"
- "I Will Call Upon the Lord"
- "Lord, I Lift Your Name on High"

Leader TiP

If you choose to not use slides or videos, you can add an element of intensity to the reading by playing an appropriate instrumental soundtrack in the background . Select music that will not divert the attention of your students. Possible selections might include tracks from Phil Keaggy's more mellow CDs. Or you could use pianist Liz Story's *My Foolish Heart* (Windham Hill Records).

Reflective Reading

"God Draws Close" Readers Theater

(15 minutes)

Ask for four volunteers to lead the group in this next worship experience. Then say: **Though God is far above us, God wants us to know and respond to him. Together, let's participate in a readers theater. Our four readers will lead us in considering how God has drawn close to us, and when they say, "We praise you, Lord" we'll respond with, "We praise you, Lord." Let's all stand, and please raise your hands in praise when you say, "We praise you, Lord."**

(Note: Raising hands in worship may already be a part of your worship tradition. If not, consider trying it on this occasion. You'll involve your students as they wait for their cues, and give them a new and positive worship experience as they involve their bodies as well as their minds in this reading.)

Have your four leaders guide the group through the "God Draws Close" script (pp. 56-57). After the reading, say: **God is high above us, but God has drawn near to us—first through creation, then through his law. He gave us the prophets. He sent his Son. And he has given us his Holy Spirit. God is pursuing a loving relationship with each of us—with each of you. Quietly reflect for one minute on one way God has made himself known to you. In a few moments I'll ask you to briefly share it with us. Join me in silent reflection.**

After one minute, ask for anyone who has a story or incident to share to do so. End by saying: **One more time, let's give God glory for all he has done.**

Leader TiP

Consider holding this communion service by candlelight, and playing Gregorian chants in the background. You can probably find a copy of the appropriate music by visiting the library and asking for a copy of *Chant* or *Chant II* by the Benedictine Monks of Santo Domingo de Silos (Angel).

Symbolic Worship

Christmas Communion

(10 minutes)

Close your time of worship with a communion service that celebrates how God is both above us and willing to draw close to us. Involve the appropriate clergy, but reserve as much of the service as possible for your students to lead.

Gather your students around a manger scene (if seasonally appropriate, an outside manger scene is ideal). You'll need a Bible, elements of the Lord's Supper, and if necessary a member of the clergy to serve the Lord's Supper at the appropriate time.

Begin by asking a student to read John 1:1-5, 10-14 aloud.

Say: **The baby we see in the manger was not always a baby in a manger. Jesus is God—and it was his hand that sent the galaxies spinning in distant space. He is all-powerful and all-knowing. Let's share one-word prayers to Jesus, who is high above all people.**

Encourage students to share one-word prayers. Among the words you might hear are "majestic," "powerful," or "mighty."

Ask a volunteer to read Isaiah 9:6-7 aloud. Then say: **When the law failed to change our hearts, God sent Jesus to be a sacrifice for our sins and to reconcile us to God the Father. This baby we see is God's loving decision to invade history and draw close to us. Let's share one-word prayers to Jesus, who has drawn close to us.**

Encourage students to share one-word prayers. Among the words you might hear are "giving," "loving," or "thanks."

Say: **About thirty years after this baby arrived in Bethlehem, a grown-up Jesus sat with his followers in an upstairs room, eating a Passover feast.**

Ask a volunteer to read Luke 22:15-20 aloud. Then say: **God is high above us, and God has drawn near to us. The Lord's Supper is a reminder of both truths. Let's share it together and worship God.**

Celebrate the Lord's Supper together. After the communion, say: **Among the first visitors to see Jesus in Bethlehem were shepherds, summoned by an angelic choir. The Bible says they left the stable rejoicing and telling others about what had happened. Why? Because they knew Jesus was here!**

Let's do the same. Let's take a few moments now to shake everyone's hand and say, "Jesus is with us!" And be happy about it—it's good news!

Encourage students to mingle and shake hands or hug saying, "Jesus is with us!"

Leader Tip

Here are some possible visual ideas you can suggest that kids use in creating a slide show or video to go along with the "God Draws Close" readers theater (pp. 56-57). The ideas are numerically keyed to various sections of the script.
1. Earth, as viewed from space
2. Nature: mountains or the sea
3. Close up of a leaf or other natural object
4. Bible
5. Luxury goods
6. Luxury goods
7. Hands washing under a stream of water
8. Upstretched hand
9. Hand holding a stone
10. Close up of an artist's rendition of Jesus' face
11. Cross
12. Dove, open sky, or other similar symbol
13. Awesome natural scenery
14. Close up of words in the Bible
15. Man kneeling in prayer
16. Jesus' face
17. People with arms around each other

God Draws Close

Reader 1 (1)	For speaking all we see and know into existence, we praise you, Lord.
All	We praise you, Lord.
Reader 2 (2)	For the earth and all it gives us, for the endless skies above us, and the beauty we see in your universe, we praise you, Lord.
All	We praise you, Lord.
Reader 4 (3)	Forgive us when we fail to care for the works of your hands, Lord. When we look at your creation and see only the creation—and not the majesty of the Creator who shaped them. We praise you, Lord.
All	We praise you, Lord.
Reader 4 (4)	For revealing your law to us through your servant Moses, we thank you, Lord.
Reader 3	For loving us enough to draw close to us through your law, for telling us how to become sons and daughters who honor your Name, we praise you, Lord.
All	We praise you, Lord.
Reader 2 (5)	Yet we are like those who, even as you proclaimed your commandments, created a golden calf and bowed down to worship it. We have turned aside from your way to follow gods of our own making.
Reader 1	We break your commandments to pursue pleasure, popularity, and self-importance.
Reader 3 (6)	We break your commandments to chase after money and those things it will buy.
Reader 4 (7)	But your forgiveness is a fountain, Lord. And for letting us come and drink of it through your Son, Jesus, we praise you, Lord.
All	We praise you, Lord.
Reader 1 (8)	For drawing close to us by raising up prophets who faithfully carried your message…
Reader 2	For calling your people back to yourself…
Reader 3	For making your will and your word known…
Reader 4	For being faithful to every promise you've made, we praise you, Lord.

All	We praise you, Lord.
Reader 1 (9)	For commending your servant Jeremiah because he spoke the truth…
Reader 4	For preserving your servant Elijah…
Reader 3	For speaking your word through Joel, Hosea, Ezekiel, and Jonah, we praise you, Lord.
All	We praise you, Lord.
Reader 4 (10)	We praise you for drawing close to us through the person of Jesus, your Son.
Reader 3	Jesus, who confronted the same passions and temptations we face, yet did not sin.
Reader 2	Jesus, who walked alongside us, showing us how to live lives pleasing to you.
Reader 1 (11)	Jesus, who faced torture and a bloody execution, but still chose to do what you wanted, so we could be drawn close to you.
Reader 4	For Jesus' willing sacrifice on our behalf, we praise you, Lord.
All	We praise you, Lord.
Reader 3 (12)	For sending your Holy Spirit to comfort and guide us, we are grateful.
Reader 2	For drawing close to us as you dwell with us in the person of the Holy Spirit, we praise you, Lord.
All	We praise you, Lord.
Reader 1 (13)	You have done so much to draw close to us, Lord. For the might and power we see demonstrated in your astounding creation, we praise you, Lord.
All	We praise you, Lord.
Reader 1 (14)	For drawing close to us by revealing yourself through your law, we praise you, Lord.
All	We praise you, Lord.
Reader 2 (15)	For drawing close to us by speaking through your prophets, we praise you, Lord.
All	We praise you, Lord.
Reader 3 (16)	For drawing close to us by sending your Son to redeem us, we praise you, Lord.
All	We praise you, Lord.
Reader 4 (17)	And for dwelling here among us in the person of your Holy Spirit, we praise you, Lord.
All	We praise you, Lord.
Reader 1	We praise you, Lord.
All	We praise you, Lord.

The Lord who Loves us unconditionally

Worship Themes:
God is love.
God's love is unconditional.

Worship Scriptures:
Romans 8:38-39

Worship Overview:
God's love is unconditional. There is nothing a person can do that will keep God's love from reaching him or her. That is not to say that God approves of all of our actions. Every person does things that damage or break his or her relationship with God. The amazing thing is that God is able to "forgive and forget" as a result of Christ's death and resurrection.

This worship service guides kids to focus on God's unconditional love by exploring God's forgiveness in the light of Christ's sacrifice for our sins. The worship experiences also challenge kids to explore God's love in light of the common elements of relationship we share with both God and other people—communication, gift giving, confession and forgiveness, celebration, serving, and even fun. All of these are expressions of God's unconditional love. And all of them can be aspects of worship to God.

Supply Checklist

- a large heart-shaped candy box or a paper cutout of a heart
- soft instrumental music on CD or cassette and a CD or cassette player
- markers

- various colors of papers
- photocopies of the "Letter From God" handout (p. 65) for each person

- candle
- tape

- newsprint

- index cards

- telephone (does not need to work)

- pens
- photocopies of the "Love Stories" handout (p. 66) for every six to eight people
- matches

Use this worship experience to help kids accept God's awesome love, and learn to praise him for loving them unconditionally.

Worship Preparation:

Select worship songs that are appropriate for your group.

Review the first dialogues in each section plus the beginning of the worship section called "A Plea for Help." Adapt these sections so they are believable and natural to your own situation in life and personality.

worShip ServiCe
Worship Introduction

A Plea for Help
(10 minutes)

Say: **Before we start, I need your help. I have to come up with a really romantic evening. I have to tell you that my mind just hasn't been very creative lately. I've got to figure something out by tomorrow. All I could come up with was a movie and dinner. Plus I've got to do it on very little money.**

I know many of you spend a lot more time thinking about dates than I do. At least you watch a lot more movies than I do. You are also experts on not having a lot of money. I guess I should give you one other piece of information. Without going into detail, I did something on the stupid side, and I really need to say I'm sorry about it. So help me out with some ideas. Where should I go? What should we do? What are some little things I could do to show I care?

Suggestions may include: renting a canoe at a park, going to a theme park, playing miniature golf, finding a quiet spot to sit and talk, cooking a homemade dinner, writing a poem, lip-syncing a song from a CD outside his or her door, or creating coupons that include things like a free car wash or an hour of uninterrupted listening.

Review the suggestions given, then say: **So what I hear you saying is that some of the key elements I need to thing about in this relationship are communication, gift giving, service, celebration, eating together, having fun, confession, and forgiveness.**

Write those elements on a sheet of newsprint, and tape the newsprint to the wall. Then say: **When trying to meet someone, I have to admit, I always get a little nervous. Sometimes I pick up the phone and call, but I always wonder what I am going to get on the other end. I think I am afraid that the person may reject me in some way. But there has always been one number I can call and know I will always be accepted and listened to.**

Pick up a phone and dial 1-800-LORD, saying the numbers out loud as you do so.

Say: **Hi, God, this is** (name). **Say, I'm here with my group, and we were just talking about relationships. I realize that I haven't talked to you for** awhile and thought maybe we should spend some time together. They were telling me about relationships and how important things like communication, gift giving, confession and forgiveness, service, celebration, eating together, and just having fun are to a relationship. What's that God? You say these are some of the same types of things that are important in our relationship with you? *(Pause.)* Yes, I'll tell them. Thanks, God, I'll talk to you soon. 'Bye now.

Hey group, God wanted me to remind you that he loves you. In fact, God wanted you to know that "neither death nor life, neither angels nor demons, neither the present nor the future, nor any powers, neither height nor depth, nor anything else in all creation, will be able to separate us from the love of God" (Romans 8:38-39). God's love is unconditional. Nothing can ever separate us from it.

Celebrative Songs

Called to Worship
(5 minutes)

Have kids prepare to worship God with singing. But before the singing begins, proclaim with enthusiasm: **This is a worship service of love. Just like the great suggestions you gave, we now come together to celebrate, serve, confess, forgive, for honest conversation, to laugh, to support, to love and be loved unconditionally by our creator God.**

Choose a couple of upbeat, fun songs that your group responds to well. Here are some suggestions.
- "I Will Call Upon the Lord"
- "Awesome God"
- "Ain't No Rock"
- "Jesus Is the Rock"

Have kids stand for the celebration time. After about five minutes of singing, ask kids to return to their seats.

Worship Reflection

Letter Reading
(15 minutes)

Say: **Take a moment and reflect on the most important relationships in your life and the various elements that make up those relationships.**

Have kids reflect on these questions:
- **How is your relationship with God similar to your other relationships? How is it different?**
- **How do you normally feel about worshiping God as a part of your relationship with him?**
- **What is it that makes worship a meaningful experience for you?**

While kids are thinking, place a large cutout heart or a large heart-shaped candy box in the front of the room. Place a lit candle in front of the heart. You may want to have a recording of some soft instrumental music ready to play in the background.

After the time of reflection, say: **I love to get mail. The first thing I do when I come home is check the mailbox. It always feels good to know that someone is thinking of me. I'm excited to share with you a letter that is addressed to us. It's a love letter for each of you.**

Dim the lights, and start the music. Ask the group to focus on the candle and the heart as you slowly read to them the "Letter From God" (p. 65). After the reading, leave a time of silence for people to sit quietly and reflect. Keep the candle lit for later activities.

Close the reflection time with a soft song such as "Seek Ye First" or "Humble Thyself in the Sight of the Lord."

Reflective Remembrances
Telling Our Own Love Stories
(15 minutes)

Adapt the following to fit your own story.

Say: **Whenever I get involved in a relationship of any kind, I discover that I must experience many different feelings...infatuation when we first met...embarrassment when I spilled my coffee on her (or him)...excitement when we went out on our first date...disappointment when I found out she (or he) had a steady boyfriend/girlfriend...hope when they broke up...fear when our relationship started getting serious...hurt when he (or she) found out I had lied about being sick...forgiven when I found out we were still friends.**

I have had a chance to share some of my "love story" with you. In our worship service we are hearing about the greatest love of all. All relationships take us through many types of feelings. But what is different about my relationship with God is that God is always ready to love me, no matter what I go through. I may have times of doubt, fear, joy, excitement, or even indifference. No matter what, God still loves me.

Now I'll give you a chance to share some of your love stories about God.

Form groups of eight or fewer, and ask groups to sit in circles on the floor. Assign each group a leader, and give the leaders each a copy of the "Love Stories" handout (p. 66). Give each group about fifteen index cards, then ask the group to brainstorm a list of feelings that commonly happen in relationships. Have them use markers to write one "feeling" word on each index card, then lay the cards in the center of the circle where everyone can see them.

Ask each person to choose a small marker to use, for example, a ring, a coin, an earring, a key, a pen cap or some other object that they may have with them.

When groups have finished listing their "feeling" words and have spread them out on the floor, say: **Facilitators, take your group through the handout, following the directions provided. When you're finished, pray together, thanking God for giving each of us "love stories" we can share.**

Symbolic Prayers

An Offering to God
(10 Minutes)

After the story-sharing experience, gather kids back together and say: **When I like somebody, I often give her (or him) something on her birthday or at Christmas. When I really, really like somebody I find myself giving gifts all the time, just to let that person know I appreciate her. Candy, flowers, little notes, cards, favorite songs, poems, even pictures of me! I sometimes get a little carried away.**

There is also a time for gift giving in our relationship with God. It is one way we can let God know how much we appreciate him. Sometimes we only think of giving money. But in our worship service, I want us to consider other things we might want to give.

Give each person a copy of the "Letter From God" (p. 65). In the second paragraph of that letter, the verses reflect ways that God wants people to respond to his love. Reread that paragraph to the group.

Hand out the colored paper and pens. Invite the group members to create their offering by simply placing pens on their paper and writing. Encourage the group to write from their hearts and not to think too hard about the mechanics of writing. It may come out as expressions of feelings, love, a promise, or a change in one's life. It may take the form of a letter, a poem, or even a drawing.

As people finish, encourage the rest of the group to remain silent. When everyone is finished, explain to group members that what they have just created are prayers. Invite students to go one at a time towards the area with the candle and the large heart. Encourage those who wish to read their prayers out loud. If some of the prayers are private, let members pause by the candle and heart as they reflect on their prayers silently.

Closing Declaration

Confession and Forgiveness
(5 Minutes)

Say: **As you shared together during the last exercise, you may have talked about some times when you didn't feel close to God or felt you had broken your relationship with God. But God is willing to love us—no matter what.**

Ask the students to each close their eyes while holding a clenched fist out in front of them. Say: **Let this clenched fist represent the hurts, pains, and mistakes of life.**

Ask the students to each remember some of the times someone hurt them, or times they made mistakes that hurt another person. Say: **Remember times when thoughts were unclean, when someone was ignored, when God was ignored, or any time that a relationship with another or God was not right. Imagine the hurts and brokenness all being held in your tightly clenched fist.**

While kids hold this position, explain that you will use your index finger to draw the outline of a heart on somebody's forehead. When you do, that person may open his or her fist and eyes. Then that person may quietly turn to two other people and draw the heart on their foreheads. This will start a chain of people repeating the same act until everyone in the room has been "released."

When everyone's eyes are open, have kids form a circle. Then say: **In the midst of all the hurts, disappointments, mistakes, frustrations, and broken relationships, may the symbol of the heart, a symbol of God's unconditional love be felt on your forehead inflaming your own heart with God's love and forgiveness.**

"For I am convinced that neither death nor life, neither angels nor demons, neither the present nor the future, nor any powers, neither height nor depth, nor anything else in all creation, will be able to separate us from the love of God that is in Christ Jesus our Lord" (Romans 8:38-39).

A Letter From God

Dear_____,

I want you to know how I feel about you so I thought I'd send you this letter to let you know that I am gracious, slow to anger, and abounding in love and faithfulness. (Exodus 34:6) It is my desire that neither height nor depth, nor anything else in all creation, will be able to separate us. (Romans 8:39) Make my joy complete by being like-minded, having the same love, being one in spirit and purpose. (Philippians 2:2) Dear friends, let us love one another. (1 John 3:18) Remain in me, and I will remain in you. No branch can bear fruit by itself; it must remain in the vine. Neither can you bear fruit unless you remain in me. (John 15:4) Greater love has no one than this, that he lay down his life for his friends. (John 15:13)

I ask in return that you love me with all your heart, and with all your soul, and with all your strength (Deuteronomy 6:5) and that you love your neighbor as yourself. (Luke 10:27) As I have loved you, so you must love one another. (John 13:34) Act justly, and...love mercy, and...walk humbly with me. (Micah 6:8) Love must be sincere. Hate what is evil; cling to what is good. (Romans 12:9) And over all...put on love, which binds...all together in perfect unity. (Colossians 3:14)

Be still, and know that I am God; I will be exalted among the nations, I will be exalted in the earth. (Psalm 46:10) Don't let anyone look down on you because you are young, but set an example for the believers in speech, in life, in love, in faith and in purity. (1 Timothy 4:12)

Never will I leave you; never will I forsake you. (Hebrews 13:5) But let him who boasts boast about this: that he understands and knows me, that I am the Lord, who exercises kindness, justice and righteousness on earth, for in these I delight. (Jeremiah 9:24)

Love,
God

Love Stories

Have group members complete each statement below by placing their markers on one of the "feeling" words on the floor. After you read each statement, ask one or two group members to share a story that illustrates their answer.

When I think of a time I've sensed God's love, I feel...

When I think of a time God seemed far away, I feel...

When I think of God's unconditional love I feel...

When I think of a cross I feel...

When I think of sin, I feel...

When I think of mercy, I feel...

When I think of my love for God, I feel...

The Lord who wants to know us

Worship Themes:
God is personal.
God invites us into a relationship with him.

Worship Scriptures:
Genesis 18:23-33; Exodus 32:7-14; 1 Kings 3:5-14; Mark 14:32-42; 2 Corinthians 12:7-9

Worship Overview:
Most of us begin life thinking of God as something like a celestial parent. There's nothing wrong with that, and it's probably inevitable. God is like Dad in many ways, or is it that Dad is like God? Enter the theologians.

But as we grow older, our view of God becomes whatever we want—an idea or a consciousness or a comet on the far side of Mars. Who cares what the Bible says about God? Those old people "created" God in their image; now it's our turn. Or is it?

The God who reveals himself in the Bible invites us into a relationship with him through prayer, study, meditation, and obedience. God wants us to live as though he were actually God. Because God is.

This worship service is an experience in talking with God, singing praises to God, and listening to God. It's an opportunity to remember that God really does love you and care about you. So have fun. Open up. Let the Spirit of God be your guide.

Supply Checklist

- Bibles
- CD or cassette player
- photocopies of the "Talking With God" handout (p. 71)

- paper
- a campfire, a candle, or a small barbecue grill

- a recording of your idea of "heavenly" music (such as a recording of harp music, classical guitar, or piano)
- markers or pens

Worship Preparation:
Before the service, choose the songs you want to sing during the worship time. As the final song in your opening worship time, sing "When I Survey the Wondrous Cross" or something similar. The song can be found in most hymnals, and it provides a nice lead-in to the worship service.

You can lead this worship experience inside or outside, but you will need a worship space where you can keep the lighting low and have the "mood" music occur on cue. The light source could be a campfire; a nice, large candle centrally located; or it could simply be low lighting or even moonlight on a night with a full moon.

Worship Service
Opening Celebration
God Is Personal
(15 minutes)

Begin with some praise songs. Try to choose some that are upbeat at first, then gradually move toward songs that are slower and more contemplative. Here are some possible songs.

- "As the Deer"
- "Father, I Adore You"
- "Create in Me a Clean Heart"
- "Victory Chant"
- "Humble Thyself in the Sight of the Lord"
- "Awesome God"

The final song will set the mood for the entire service. If possible, sing the hymn "When I Survey the Wondrous Cross" or something similar.

After the song ends say: **It was almost two thousand years ago, and there were three crosses set up on a hill outside the city of Jerusalem. They were crucifixion crosses—execution crosses. Each cross was occupied by a dirty, beat-up, blood-encrusted man. The eyes of the first man flashed with anger and hatred. Those of the third man gleamed with fear and the realization that death was near. The eyes of the one in the middle were filled with sorrow...and love.**

As members of the crowd threw traditional taunts and jeers their way, each reacted in kind. The angry criminal berated the occupant of the middle cross for the promises he had made during his lifetime. "If you really are the Messiah, save yourself and us!" he cried. The fearful one stopped him, "This is no time for that!" he said. "Don't you know we are about to die?" Then he turned to the central figure, looked deep into his eyes and begged, "Jesus, remember me when you come into your kingdom." And Jesus answered him, "Today you will be with me in paradise."

We need not wait as long as the thief on the cross before accepting God's invitation into a relationship with him. That criminal's life was nearly over when he realized who Jesus was. There was no time for him to be baptized, to learn about Jesus, to come to know Jesus. He would be dead in only a few hours, never having moved from the spot where Jesus welcomed him into his kingdom. But he was welcomed.

For us it is different. We have the opportunity to live our lives with Jesus. We don't have to wait until our deathbed. We can begin right now. Or if we've

already begun, we can strengthen our relationship with God as we worship him together.

Ask:

● **Why do you think it's important for us to know God personally?**

Worshipful Reflection

The God of Relationships

(15 minutes)

Form groups of three or four, and give each group a Bible and one section of the "Talking With God" handout (p. 71). It's OK if more than one group gets the same section of the handout. Give the groups time to look up their passages and answer the questions, then bring them back together and have volunteers tell about their group's person. Then say: **It may not be possible for anyone here to be an Abraham, Moses, Solomon, or Paul, but we can strengthen our relationship with God by learning to talk with God as freely as they did, and by focusing on Jesus and living with him as a constant companion every day.**

Symbolic Worship

Walking With Jesus

(20 minutes)

Start the "heavenly music" you chose before the worship service. As the music begins, distribute paper and markers or pens.

Say: **Want to think of God? Picture Jesus. Want a closer walk with God? Walk with Jesus.**

Listen to the music, and allow your imagination to draw for you a picture of Jesus, focusing on whatever attribute of his that you like. *(Pause.)* **Now transfer your thought-picture to your paper. Artists might draw an image. Others might simply want to use words or sentences to focus on him. Allow the music to help you. Please don't talk or critique another's work.**

After three or four minutes, say: **Keep listening to the music as you focus your thoughts on the image of Jesus you have made.** *(Pause.)* **Remember, your creation is merely an aid to help you concentrate on Jesus.** *(Pause.)* **Now speak to him and thank him for your friends, for your parents, for health, and for knowing him as Lord.** *(Pause.)* **Thank him for promising never to leave you.** *(Pause.)* **Ask him whatever is on your heart at this time, and close with an "amen."**

Have kids form pairs, then distribute paper and pens to each person. Say: **Jesus wants to build a strong relationship with you. But sometimes we don't feel close to God, and it seems like Jesus is nowhere around. Tell your partner about a time you felt like God was distant or unapproachable.**

After kids share, tell the partners to write a prayer to God for their friend in response to his or her story. For example, someone might write, "Lord Jesus, I pray that you will let Sara know that you are with her all the time—especially when she feels lonely or depressed about life." When everyone is finished, have kids fold their prayers and focus their attention back on you.

Declarative Worship

Lifting Prayers to God

(5 minutes)

Point to the candle (or campfire or barbecue grill) and say: **God's people have used the smoke of burning incense to symbolize their prayers rising to God for thousands of years. First the Jews, then Christians used—and some still use—this symbolism. Let's use the same symbol now to represent the prayers we're offering to God.**

Have kids each place their prayers into the fire one at a time. Then say: **As the smoke from our burning prayers rises heavenward, so our requests will rise to the throne of Grace where our loving God hears and answers them with the answers that he knows are best for us.**

Join with me now in praying the prayer Jesus taught as we conclude this worship service.

Lead kids in praying in unison the Lord's Prayer found in Matthew 6:9-13.

☎ Talking With God

1. Genesis 18:23-33—Abraham Bargains With God

- Why was Abraham bargaining with God?
- How many righteous people would it require for God to spare the city?
    …at the beginning of the bargaining?
    …at the end of the bargaining?
- Have you ever thought of God as someone you could bargain with? Why or why not?

---

2. Exodus 32:7-14—Moses Pleads With God

- Why was Moses pleading with God?
- What argument did Moses use to get God to change his mind?
- Have you ever thought of God as someone who could change his mind?

---

3. 1 Kings 3:5-14—God Offers Solomon Anything He Wants

- What did Solomon ask for?
- Why did he ask for that?
- What would you ask God for if he promised to give you anything?

---

4. Mark 14:32-42—Jesus Prays in the Garden

- Why was Jesus troubled?
- What did he mean by "this cup"?
- Why doesn't God always give us the answer we want when we pray?

---

5. 2 Corinthians 12:7-9—Paul Requests Healing for Himself

- What did Paul pray for?
- Why had he been given this "thorn in the flesh"?
- What did he decide to do after God refused to take the "thorn" away?
- How can you follow Paul's example?

God gives us his Spirit

The Lord who Gives us His Spirit

Worship Themes:
God is Spirit.
God gave us his Spirit.

Worship Scriptures:
Lamentations 3:23; Psalms 23:6; 37:7; John 3:16; 14:27; Acts 1:5-8; 2:1-4, 17, 21; Romans 11:22; Galatians 5:22-23; Philippians 4:4-5; and 2 Timothy 1:7

Worship Overview:
Jesus promised us that he would never leave us and that he would send his Spirit to comfort us and be with us always. In a world where kids often feel powerless under trying circumstances, the Holy Spirit is available to be our power. The Spirit of Jesus is living inside the heart of each Christian, gently guiding us in the way we should go.

This worship service helps students celebrate the awesome coming of the Holy Spirit to the world. It will also challenge your kids to honor God's gift by living out their daily lives full of the "fruit" of his Spirit—love, joy, peace, patience, kindness, goodness, faithfulness, gentleness and self-control.

Use this worship experience to help kids worship God for giving them his Spirit and examine the fruit of the Spirit in their lives.

Supply Checklist

- Bibles
- a CD or tape of rushing wind
- words and music for worship songs
- one pack of fruit candy or a bowl of cut-up fruit for every five people
- "praying hands" stickers
- matches
- tape
- a CD or cassette player
- twelve candles
- two copies of the "Fruit of the Spirit" reading (p. 77)
- a recording of a song that focuses on living out your faith, such as "Show Yourselves to Be"
- poster board
- markers

Supply Checklist

Worship Preparation:
Before the service, select your worship songs for the singing time.

Set up the CD or cassette player and cue up the song you chose that focuses on living out your faith or demonstrating the fruit of the Spirit.

Recruit and coach your reader for the opening worship experience so he or she will know when and what to read. It might help to take ten minutes before the worship to run through the reading with him or her. The opening reading is dramatic and should be read powerfully by someone who is comfortable with public reading.

Visit your library to secure a copy of the "rushing wind" sound effect. Or if you prefer, sound effects tapes or CDs can be purchased at most music stores. You can also make a sound effect tape yourself by recording your own simulated "rushing wind" sound on a tape recorder.

For the opening worship experience, darken the worship area (use foil or heavy cloth to cover windows if necessary). Place twelve candles at various places around the room. Provide matches to a few volunteers, and ask them to light the candles on your cue during the opening worship experience.

Use poster board and markers to make nine "fruit" signs for your worship area—one for each fruit of the Spirit. Make sure the words are large enough to be seen by everyone. Place them face down all over the floor of the worship area.

Prepare the bowls of cut-up fruit for the closing activity and display them in the worship area as a visual aid. Or if time is short, you can substitute packs of fruit-flavored candy instead.

Worship Service
Symbolic Celebration
Rushing Wind
(15 minutes)

As kids enter the darkened worship area, tell them to remain totally silent and be seated. Have your first reader read aloud Acts 1:5-8. Just as he or she finishes, start the "rushing wind" sound effect. Then have the reader continue by reading aloud Acts 2:1-4. At the same time, have the candle lighters light the candles you placed around the room to symbolize the tongues of fire which appeared on the disciples heads.

Once all the candles are lit, have the reader continue by reading aloud Acts 2:17, 21. When he or she finishes, fade out the "rushing wind" sound, and go right into singing a song that praises God for his Spirit, or focuses on the fruit of the Spirit (such as "Spirit Song" or "Holy, Holy").

Before moving on to the next song, say: **Let's continue to sing to God in a way that shows him how thankful we are for the awesome gift of his Spirit. Let's sing to him with all our joy and praise!**

You also might want to sing any of the following songs.
● "I Will Call Upon the Lord"
● "More Love, More Power"
● "Arise, Oh Lord"
● "Father, I Adore You"

Worship Reflection

Seeking His Fruit

(20 minutes)

After the singing time, say: **We've celebrated and thanked God for the awesome gift of his Holy Spirit. But why?**

Ask:

● **Why did God send us the Spirit of Jesus to live in each of us?**

● **How can we live differently because of the gift?**

Say: **God's Word says that if we've received the gift of Jesus as our Savior, then we have the Spirit of Jesus living inside of us. If we have the Spirit of Jesus, how should we be living our lives? Can others see the "fruit" of Jesus alive and growing in us or do our "fruit trees" appear to be rotten and dying? Let's hear what God's Word says as our readers come forward.**

Set out tape so students can see it. Have the two readers for the "Fruit of the Spirit" reading (p. 77) get into place. As Reader 1 reads each "fruit," ask a different volunteer to find the appropriate "fruit" sign and tape it to the wall of the worship area. This experience should not be rushed; encourage students to take their time.

When all the signs are up, have the readers be seated. Then say: **God has given us his Spirit, and the fruit of his Spirit is evident in our lives. But we still sometimes struggle with living out all of the fruit of the Spirit. There are probably some qualities you see here that you just can't seem to grasp in your life. We need God's power to help to us grow stronger in the Spirit, so we can display all of his fruit in our lives.**

Look around the room at the signs we've displayed. Take time to silently reflect on which aspects of the Spirit you struggle with, and pray to God for his help.

Quietly play the song, "Show Yourselves to Be" (or something similar). After a minute, hold up the praying-hands stickers and say: **When you are finished reflecting and praying, I invite you to come forward and place one of these praying-hands stickers on the appropriate fruit signs. Make this an act of commitment to allow God's Spirit to develop his fruit in you. Don't rush through this. Take your time and come forward only when you are through praying to God and seeking his help. When you're finished, be seated and silently listen to the music or pray for those around you.**

If kids are still praying when the song is over, play it again or have something else appropriate ready to play. When everyone is finished, fade out the music.

Closing Declaration

God's Fruit in You

(20 minutes)

Ask kids to quietly form groups of five or fewer with those sitting around them.
Say: **We have prayed about and committed to growing the "fruit of the Spirit"**

in areas where we fall short. Now let's celebrate the "fruit of the Spirit" in each of us that God has blessed us with.

Ask the person wearing the most "fruit basket" colors in each small group to come forward and get a bowl of fruit (or pack of fruit candy, whichever you used). Starting with the person holding the bowl, have group members each tell that person one fruit of the Spirit they see in him or her by completing this sentence: "I praise God for the fruit of _____ that I see in your life. God has been good to you!" After everyone has completed the declaration for that person, have him or her take a piece of fruit (or candy) and enjoy it! Then have that person pass the bowl to the person on the right and repeat the process. Continue until everyone in the group has received a fruit.

To close the worship time, have kids form a circle. Tell them that you're going to call out each fruit of the Spirit. Each time you do, have them respond by declaring, "God's (fruit you just named) is in me!" For example, when you say, "The fruit of the Spirit is love," kids will respond by declaring, "God's love is in me!"

Call out the following statement nine times, highlighting a different fruit of the Spirit each time. Pause after each statement to allow kids to make their declaration.

Say: **The fruit of the Spirit is...** (love, joy, peace, patience, kindness, goodness, faithfulness, gentleness, self-control)!

FRUIT OF the SPIRIT

Reader 1 For the fruit of the Spirit is love! **Reader 2** "For God so loved the world that he gave his one and only Son, that whoever believes in him shall not perish but have eternal life." (John 3:16) **Reader 1** Joy! **Reader 2** "Rejoice in the Lord always. I will say it again: Rejoice!" (Philippians 4:4) **Reader 1** Peace! **Reader 2** "Peace I leave with you; my peace I give you…Do not let your hearts be troubled and do not be afraid." (John 14:27) **Reader 1** Patience! **Reader 2** "Be still before the Lord and wait patiently for him." (Psalm 37:7) **Reader 1** Kindness! **Reader 2** "Consider therefore the kindness and sternness of God: sternness to those who fell, but kindness to you, provided that you continue in his kindness." (Romans 11:22) **Reader 1** Goodness! **Reader 2** "Surely goodness and love will follow me all the days of my life." (Psalm 23:6) **Reader 1** Faithfulness! **Reader 2** "Great is your faithfulness." (Lamentations 3:23) **Reader 1** Gentleness! **Reader 2** "Let your gentleness be evident to all." (Philippians 4:5) **Reader 1** and Self-Control! **Reader 2** "For God did not give us a spirit of timidity, but a spirit of power, of love and of self-discipline." (2 Timothy 1:7)

The Lord Who Is Present

Worship Themes:

God is present everywhere.
God is always with us.

Worship Scriptures:

Deuteronomy 33:27; Psalms 23:4; 46:1; 103:13-14;139:1-18, 23-24; Isaiah 42:16; John 15:13; Hebrews 13:8; 1 Peter 2:9; and Revelation 21:6

Worship Overview:

From infancy, we learn to expect the world around us to pay attention to us. Our needs, our appetites, our welfare, and our comfort take precedence over everything. Too often we carry that expectation into our adult lives.

True worship begins when we realize that we are not at the center of the universe. When we are faced with the awesome character of God, we realize our inward attention must be turned outward. Then we reflect on the wonder, the mystery, and the transcendence of God, who is everywhere present and greater than anything we can express.

Psalm 139 is one of the great prayers of the Bible that expresses the balance of an awesome reverence toward God and a trusting, understanding friendship with him. This service will help your kids understand this balance—worshiping God for his wonder and majesty, and thanking him for being so close and interested in every detail of their lives. Use this worship experience to help your kids understand what God's presence means in their lives.

Supply Checklist

- Bibles
- a videotape created by youth leader or several group members
- a candle and matches for each participant (or battery powered candles)
- pens or pencils
- envelopes

- marker
- newsprint
- paper
- a CD or cassette recording of a song that expresses the idea that God is close.

- a VCR
- a CD or cassette player
- a television

Worship Preparation:

Before the service, prepare the praise songs to be used during the "Celebration" time.

Prepare a videotape to be used during the service. This could be done by the leaders or several of the kids. The scenes in the video will correspond to verses of Psalm 139. (See the following suggestions.) While the video is played during the service, turn the volume off, and have students read aloud the appropriate verses. That way you'll avoid unwanted background noise on the video, and you'll be able to edit the scenes together more easily.

Here are some suggestions for scenes for the video.

● Psalm 139:1-5—a scene showing a student at school, sitting in her desk, walking down the hall, raising her hand, and so on

● Psalm 139:7-10—a scene showing the panorama of the countryside, the vastness of the sky, or a sunrise

● Psalm 139:11-13—a scene showing light illuminating the darkness. Perhaps this could be a candle burning in a completely dark room, or a dark room being illuminated by a dimmer switch

● Psalm 139:14-16—a scene showing a newborn baby

● Psalm 139:17-18—a scene with someone reading a Bible while walking along a lake shore

● Psalm 139:23-24—a scene showing someone standing with hands spread as though inviting God to search him

Make sure to have the video cued for viewing. Also have the candles ready and the cassette tape or CD cued.

Worship Service
Declarative Celebration

The Lord Who Is Present
(15 minutes)

Begin the service by having the kids sit in a completely dark room. Say: **Today we are beginning this worship service in the dark to help you remember a time when you were entirely alone. Think about how it felt.**

Ask kids to reflect on these questions:

● **Why were you alone?**

● **Why had your friends or family left you in that situation?**

● **What was it like being in the dark—as you are right now?**

Turn on the lights and say: **In this service we are going on a quest to recognize the presence of God in our lives. We are not alone. We want to worship him for being present *everywhere*, and we want to thank him for being present *with us*. Let's begin by singing songs that give him joyful praise.**

Lead the group in several songs, beginning with more upbeat songs and ending with a softer, more reflective song. For example, you might sing these songs.

● "Joy!"

● "Lord, I Lift Your Name on High"

● "We're Here to Praise You"

After singing these songs, instruct kids that real worship means praising God for who God is and what God has done for us. It means singing his praises with joy and sharing aloud specific ways that God is great to us *personally.* Ask kids to speak one-sentence declarations of how God is great by completing this sentence: "God is so great to *me* because…" Before the kids speak, offer an example by saying something like, "God is so great to *me* because I can go to him in prayer any time, and I know God will listen."

After several students have spoken, ask the students to sing "Thou Art Worthy." Encourage kids to close their eyes and sing the words directly to God from their hearts.

Creative Reflection

David's Psalm

(20 minutes)

After singing, ask the kids to listen while you briefly tell them about two aspects of God's presence. Write the words "transcendence" and "intimacy" along with the definitions of each one on newsprint so that all can see. (Transcendence means to excel or go beyond. Intimacy means to be familiar or close to someone or something.)

Then say: **When we think about God's presence with us, we can understand it in two ways. First of all, we can describe it as being transcendent. That means that it excels; it goes beyond or surpasses anything that we can describe. For example, God's presence transcends time. Can you express in your own words what that means?**

Wait for response, and then ask two kids to read aloud Hebrews 13:8 and Revelation 21:6.

Say: **God's presence also transcends location. Can you express in your own words what that means?** Wait for response, and then ask one student to read aloud Psalm 23:4.

Say: **God's presence also transcends circumstances. Can you express in your own words what that means?** Wait for response and then ask two of the kids to read aloud Psalm 46:1 and Deuteronomy 33:27.

Say: **The other word that describes God's presence is intimacy. Intimacy means familiar or close. To be intimate is to be a friend or a confidant. That's what God is to us.**

Have two kids read aloud Psalm 103:13-14 and John 15:13. Then ask:

● **How does it make you feel to know that God is always with you?**

● **If God is close like a friend, what can you expect from him?**

Say: **One of the great prayers of the Bible was written by David. David was amazed that God was so great, and that his presence could transcend all of the boundaries that could even be thought up in David's mind. But what impressed David most was the knowledge that God intimately knew him and was present with him. Watch and listen to the videotape of David's prayer.**

Show the videotape that was prepared beforehand of Psalm 139. Then form groups of three to four, and have groups discuss these questions:

Leader Tip

If you are unable to make a videotape for this part of the service, you can have kids act out the psalm while you read it. Either ask a few volunteers to act out the psalm while you read it aloud, or have the whole class participate. Then continue the worship experience as written.

- How does it make you feel to know that God knows everything about your life?
- What are you facing in your life that makes you happy that God is with you?
- When you hear that you were "woven" or "knit" together by God, how does that make you feel?
- Are there times when you wish God was not present? Explain.

Ask the students to remain in their groups for the next portion of the worship service. Then distribute candles and matches to each person.

"For you created my inmost being; you knit me together in my mother's womb. I praise you because I am fearfully and wonderfully made; your works are wonderful, I know that full well. My frame was not hidden from you when I was made in the secret place. When I was woven together in the depths of the earth, your eyes saw my unformed body. All the days ordained for me were written in your book before one of them came to be. How precious to me are your thoughts, O God! How vast is the sum of them! Were I to count them, they would outnumber the grains of sand. When I awake, I am still with you."

—Psalm 139:13-18

Symbolic Action

Light in the Darkness

(10 minutes)

Turn off the lights, and ask students to remember again that time they thought of when they were alone. Then play the song you picked out that expresses the idea that God is close.

After the song, say: **We are sitting here in the dark to symbolize a time when we felt alone. The darkness might be when we think that God is not anywhere near us. But when we feel that way, it's only because we have not recognized that God is present. As God's children, we have the promise that God will always be there—like a light shining in the darkness.**

One by one, light the candles in your group, and watch as the candles illuminate each face around us, the group we are in, and finally the entire room.

After the entire group has lit their candles, have several volunteers take turns reading these Scripture passages: Psalm 139:11-13; Isaiah 42:16; and 1 Peter 2:9.

After the reading, have kids discuss these questions in their groups:

● **How is the lighting of the candles like recognizing God's presence in our lives?**

● **What is the one idea you can take with you this week to be reminded of God's presence in your life?**

After the groups have reflected on this symbolic action, turn on the lights and say: **In the temple of the Old Testament, a light was always burning. This light lit up the room that held the "bread of the Presence" and it symbolized God's constant presence with his people** (Exodus 25:30 and 27:20.)

Say: **No matter how dark your life gets or how alone you feel, if you're a Christian, you have an eternal light in your heart, God will never leave you. He knows you. He knows what you think, what you say, and where you go. He knows the struggles that you are having right now. And he wants each of you to reach out to him and ask for help in your struggles.**

But sometimes we run away from God's presence and we don't want his help. Sometimes we don't want him to know us that well because we know that we have thoughts or are doing things that do not please him.

Ask the students to bow their heads and pray along with you silently as you pray: **Search me, O God, and know my heart; test me and know my anxious thoughts. See if there is any offensive way in me, and lead me in the way everlasting.**

Private Reflection

Love Notes to God

(10 minutes)

After the prayer, distribute a sheet of paper, an envelope, and a pen or pencil to each person. Then say: **True worship always asks for some kind of response in each one of us toward God. If we recognize how great God is, and we** are thankful for what he means to us, then we will try to continue our worship when we leave this place. After all, God's presence will go with us when we leave.

On their papers, ask kids to each write a letter to God expressing some things that they learned in the service. For example, suggest that kids tell God:

- something no one else knows about them.
- how they feel about God's transcendence and intimacy in their lives.
- what they will do the next time they're faced with the temptation to sin, since they know God is always with them.
- how they can help someone else know God is present with us.

When they finish their letters, have kids seal their letters in the envelopes. Encourage kids to take the letters with them when they leave, so they can read them occasionally to remind them of God's eternal presence with them.

To close the worship time, ask the kids to join hands and sing together "Awesome God." After the song, say: **May the presence of God be real in your lives this week, and may that presence give you a reason to worship the Lord.**

We should wor-
ship God in spirit
and in truth.

The Lord who Is Faithful

Worship Themes:

God is faithful.
God keeps his promises.

Worship Scriptures:

Psalm 33 and Proverbs 3:5-6

Worship Overview:

Many teenagers today have a hard time trusting in anyone or anything. They often feel let down by society, friends, even their families. This can make it difficult for teenagers to trust in a God they can't even see or hear.

The goal of this worship service is to remind the worshipers of all the promises God has made and kept to his people. Through these worship experiences, students will be encouraged to trust God with struggles they have, and allow him to guide their lives.

This worship experience helps kids see that when we trust God, he'll always direct us where we need to go.

Supply Checklist

- Bibles
- CD or cassette player

- six copies of the "Extra!" skit (pp. 89-90)
- markers
- soft instrumental music on CD or cassette

- newspapers or tabloid magazines
- a heart-shaped cutout for each person
- tape

Supply Checklist

Worship Preparation:

Before the service, recruit six people to perform the "Extra!" skit (pp. 89-90). It's very easy to do and needs only a ten-minute run-through before the service.

Choose the songs for the celebration time. Suggestions have been made for the theme and flow of this service, but you can substitute any of these for other songs you choose.

Cue-up the tape or CD as needed.

Cut one large heart from 8 1/2x11-inch paper for each person.

Worship Service

Opening Celebration

God Is Awesome

(10 minutes)

Begin the worship service by leading the group in several praise and worship songs that are upbeat and well-known. Encourage kids to praise God freely, clapping their hands as they sing. Here are three possible songs.

- "Great and Mighty Is He"
- "I Will Call Upon the Lord"
- "Awesome God"

"Sing joyfully to the Lord, you righteous; it is fitting for the upright to praise him. Praise the Lord with the harp; make music to him on the ten-stringed lyre. Sing to him a new song; play skilfully, and shout for joy. For the word of the Lord is right and true; he is faithful in all he does. The Lord loves righteousness and justice; the earth is full of his unfailing love."

—Psalm 33:1-5

Symbolic Declaration

Leader Tip

For smaller groups, form pairs for this activity.

God Is Faithful!

(40 minutes)

After the singing, have kids form groups of six or fewer. Give each group a tabloid or newspaper. Ask groups to find the "hardest to believe" story in their papers. Tell them to be ready to share why they picked the stories they did. After two minutes, call time, and have one person from each group share its hard-to-believe story and explain why the group chose it. After all the groups have shared, ask:

- **Why don't we always believe what we hear?**
- **How do we know whether something is true?**
- **How do you decide what to believe in?**
- **How do you decide who to trust?**

Say: **To some, the Bible seems to be full of hard-to-believe stories and promises. But God has always been faithful to keep every promise he has made when the time was right. As we watch our worship skit, make a mental list of some of the hard-to-believe stories and promises you hear.**

Have your actors perform the "Extra!" skit (pp. 89-90). After the skit, ask:

- **What did you put on your mental list of hard-to-believe stories or promises?**

Say: **God's Word has promised many fantastic things, and they have actually happened, but people often don't seem to notice or care. Why is that? Don't they believe? Don't they trust God to be faithful to his promises?**

Set out markers and the large heart shapes, then say: **And what about you? What are some promises God has made to us that you find hard to believe? I'd like each small group to work together and search their Bibles for five promises of God. An example is Proverbs 3:5-6, which says, "Trust in the Lord with all your heart and lean not on your own understanding; in all your ways acknowledge him, and he will make your paths straight."**

As you find a promise, stand up as a group and read it out loud for the whole group to hear. Once you've found five, write each of the promises on a separate large heart shape. Then have someone from your group tape the heart to the wall of our worship area. Declaring God's truth is a way of worshiping him. Let's declare God's promises as a way of worshiping his faithfulness.

When groups are finished, have kids each stand next to a promise that they're particularly thankful for. Have kids take turns offering a declaration to God by completing this prayer aloud: "God, I praise you for promising to (name the promise)."

When everyone is finished, say: "In Jesus' name, amen."

Silent Reflection

Committed to God

(10 minutes)

Have students quietly turn to Psalm 33. Lead the students in a responsive prayer of Psalm 33. Instruct students to read aloud the even-numbered verses, while you read aloud the odd-numbered verses. Encourage students to read the psalm as a prayer of praise to God.

Play some soft instrumental music in the background. Say: **Now that we've heard and reflected on the promises in God's Word, let's consider how those promises can impact our lives. As I ask each of the following questions, silently answer each question to God in prayer.**

Pause for thirty seconds between each question.

● **Why do you need God to be faithful to you?**

● **In what areas do you struggle to trust in God's faithfulness?**

● **What's one promise you've heard today that you will commit to believe?**

● **What's one promise you can make to God today, as an act of worship to him?**

Close the service by reading the following benediction from 1 Thessalonians 5:23-25: **"May God himself, the God of peace, sanctify you through and through. May your whole spirit, soul and body be kept blameless at the coming of our Lord Jesus Christ. The one who calls you is faithful and he will do it."**

The Characters:
Newsboy (a kid who sells papers on a street corner), Passerby One, Passerby Two, Passerby Three, Passerby Four, Passerby Five

Newsboy: *(Holds up a paper.)* Extra! Extra! Read all about it! Baby Born in Bethlehem!

(Passerby One enters and walks past without paying attention, then exits.)

Newsboy: King Comes to Lowly Stable! Hey, get your paper!

(Passerby Two enters slowly, looking around.)

Newsboy: *(Looking at Passerby Two)* Extra! Extra! Get your paper here! Amazing Star Appears in Eastern Sky! Heavenly Choir Sings to Shepherds! Wise Men Travel From Afar!

Passerby Two: Excuse me…Does your paper have the story about that movie star who walked off the set when she ran out of hair spray?

Newsboy: Uh…no.

Passerby Two: Oh. Well, never mind.

(Passerby Two exits. The Newsboy sighs and tries again.)

Newsboy: Extra! Man Turns Water Into Wine!

(Passersby Three and Four enter, pretending to talk with each other.)

Newsboy: Ten Lepers Healed! Lazarus Recovers From Fatal Illness! Get your paper here, folks!

Passerby Three: *(To Newsboy)* Do you have the really big story? About the lady who found a potato shaped like the Brazilian hockey team?

Newsboy: Well, no.

Passerby Four: What kind of paper is that? Don't you have any news in it?

(Passersby Three and Four exit. The Newsboy shakes his or her head and tries again.)

Newsboy: Hey, read all about it inside! Long-Promised Messiah Arrives! Triumphant Entry Parade Greeted by Cheering Crowds!

(Passerby Five enters and listens.)

Newsboy: *(Looking at Passerby Five)* Extra! Messiah Condemned in Illegal Trial! Scandal Taints Roman Governor!

Passerby Five: Speaking of scandal, how about that messy divorce involving a certain U.S. senator and a glamorous librarian from Slug Harbor, New Hampshire?

Newsboy: Uh…I hadn't heard about it.

Passerby Five: And you call that a newspaper? *(Exits.)*

*(The **Newsboy**, irritated, tries again.)*

Newsboy: *(Irritated, complaining)* Get your paper! Messiah Executed on Cross! Earthquake Rocks Jerusalem! Come on, folks! Read all about it!

*(**Passerby One** enters again from the other side, walks past without paying attention, and exits.)*

Newsboy: Hey, what's the matter with you people? Don't you recognize the story of the century when you hear it?

*(**Passerby One** enters again.)*

Passerby One: *(Excitedly)* Did you say the story of the century?

Newsboy: Yes!

Passerby One: You mean the one about the guy in Australia who can play "The Brady Bunch Theme" on the pipe organ with his toes?

Newsboy: No!

Passerby One: Well, then, forget it. *(Exits.)*

*(The **Newsboy** glares after him or her, then tries one more time.)*

Newsboy: OK! Maybe those stories weren't impressive enough for you. But there's no way you can resist this one! *(Pauses to roll up his or her sleeves, then calls out more loudly than ever.)* Extra! Extra! Man Rises From the Dead! Massive Stone Rolled Away by Angels! Man Walks Through Walls! Dead Man Lives Again! Eternal Life Guaranteed to All Who Believe!

*(The **Newsboy** waits hopefully, but nothing happens. Finally he or she throws the paper on the floor, disgusted.)*

Newsboy: I give up! I guess the good news…just isn't good enough anymore! *(The **Newsboy** shrugs and exits.)*

Index

Scripture Index

Group Publishing, Inc.
Attention: Product Development
P.O. Box 481
Loveland, CO 80539
Fax: (970) 669-1994

Evaluation for *AWESOME WORSHIP SERVICES FOR YOUTH*

Please help Group Publishing, Inc., continue to provide innovative and useful resources for ministry. Please take a moment to fill out this evaluation and mail or fax it to us. Thanks!

● ● ●

1. As a whole, this book has been (circle one)

not very helpful   very helpful

1   2   3   4   5   6   7   8   9   10

2. The best things about this book:

3. Ways this book could be improved:

4. Things I will change because of this book:

5. Other books I'd like to see Group publish in the future:

6. Would you be interested in field-testing future Group products and giving us your feedback? If so, please fill in the information below:

Name _____

Street Address _____

City _____ State _____ Zip _____

Phone Number _____ Date _____

core belief™
Bible Study Series

Give Your Teenagers a Solid Faith Foundation That Lasts a Lifetime!

Here are the *essentials* of the Christian life—core values teenagers *must* believe to make good decisions now...and build an *unshakable* lifelong faith. Developed by youth workers like you...field-tested with *real* youth groups in *real* churches...here's the meat your kids *must* have to grow spiritually—presented in a fun, involving way!

Each 4-session **Core Belief Bible Study Series** book lets you easily...

● Lead deep, compelling, *relevant* discussions your kids won't want to miss...
● Involve teenagers in exploring life-changing truths...
● Help kids create healthy relationships with each other—and you!

Plus you'll make an *eternal difference* in the lives of your kids as you give them a solid faith foundation that stands firm on God's Word.

Here are the Core Belief Bible Study Series titles already available...

Senior High Studies

Why **Authority** Matters	0-7644-0892-5	Why **Prayer** Matters	0-7644-0893-3
Why **Being a Christian** Matters	0-7644-0883-6	Why **Relationships** Matter	0-7644-0896-8
Why **Creation** Matters	0-7644-0880-1	Why **Serving Others** Matters	0-7644-0895-X
Why **Forgiveness** Matters	0-7644-0887-9	Why **Spiritual Growth** Matters	0-7644-0884-4
Why **God** Matters	0-7644-0874-7	Why **Suffering** Matters	0-7644-0879-8
Why **God's Justice** Matters	0-7644-0886-0	Why **the Bible** Matters	0-7644-0882-8
Why **Jesus Christ** Matters	0-7644-0875-5	Why **the Church** Matters	0-7644-0890-9
Why **Love** Matters	0-7644-0889-5	Why **the Holy Spirit** Matters	0-7644-0876-3
Why **Our Families** Matter	0-7644-0894-1	Why **the Last Days** Matter	0-7644-0888-7
Why **Personal Character** Matters	0-7644-0885-2	Why **the Spiritual Realm** Matters	0-7644-0881-X
		Why **Worship** Matters	0-7644-0891-7

Junior High/Middle School Studies

The Truth About **Authority**	0-7644-0868-2	The Truth About **Serving Others**	0-7644-0871-2
The Truth About **Being a Christian**	0-7644-0859-3	The Truth About **Sin and Forgiveness**	0-7644-0863-1
The Truth About **Creation**	0-7644-0856-9		
The Truth About **Developing Character**	0-7644-0861-5	The Truth About **Spiritual Growth**	0-7644-0860-7
The Truth About **God**	0-7644-0850-X	The Truth About **Suffering**	0-7644-0855-0
The Truth About **God's Justice**	0-7644-0862-3	The Truth About **the Bible**	0-7644-0858-5
The Truth About **Jesus Christ**	0-7644-0851-8	The Truth About **the Church**	0-7644-0899-2
The Truth About **Love**	0-7644-0865-8	The Truth About **the Holy Spirit**	0-7644-0852-6
The Truth About **Our Families**	0-7644-0870-4	The Truth About **the Last Days**	0-7644-0864-X
The Truth About **Prayer**	0-7644-0869-0	The Truth About **the Spiritual Realm**	0-7644-0857-7
The Truth About **Relationships**	0-7644-0872-0	The Truth About **Worship**	0-7644-0867-4

Exciting Resources for Your Youth Ministry

All-Star Games From All-Star Youth Leaders

The ultimate game book—from the biggest names in youth ministry! All-time no-fail favorites from Wayne Rice, Les Christie, Rich Mullins, Tiger McLuen, Darrell Pearson, Dave Stone, Bart Campolo, Steve Fitzhugh, and 21 others! You get all the games you'll need for any situation. Plus, you get practical advice about how to design your own games and tricks for turning a *good* game into a *great* game!

ISBN 0-7644-2020-8

Last Impressions: Unforgettable Closings for Youth Meetings

Make the closing moments of your youth programs powerful and memorable with this collection of Group's best-ever low-prep (or no-prep!) youth meeting closings. You get over 170 favorite closings, each tied to a thought-provoking Bible passage. Great for anyone who works with teenagers!

ISBN 1-55945-629-9

The Youth Worker's Encyclopedia of Bible-Teaching Ideas

Here are the most comprehensive idea-books available for youth workers. With more than 365 creative ideas in each of these 400-page encyclopedias, there's at least one idea for every book of the Bible. You'll find ideas for retreats and overnighters…learning games…adventures…special projects…affirmations… parties…prayers…music…devotions…skits…and more!

Old Testament   ISBN 1-55945-184-X
New Testament   ISBN 1-55945-183-1

PointMaker™ Devotions for Youth Ministry

These 45 PointMakers™ help your teenagers discover, understand, and apply biblical principles. Use PointMakers as brief meetings on specific topics or slide them into any youth curriculum to make a lasting impression. Includes handy Scripture and topical indexes that make it quick and easy to select the perfect PointMaker for any lesson you want to teach!

ISBN 0-7644-2003-8

Order today from your local Christian bookstore, or write: Group Publishing, P.O. Box 485, Loveland, CO 80539.

More Worship Resources for Your Youth Group

Worship Ideas for Youth Ministry

Your teenagers need to know—and *feel*—that God is in control of their lives. So teach your kids how to worship…and build a meaningful relationship with God. Each worship idea is based on a passage from the Gospels. Ideas include traditional forms of worship and exciting new ideas—perfect for starting youth meetings, developing a biblical theme, enjoying a special youth worship and prayer meeting…or helping youth lead an entire congregation in worship!

ISBN 0-7644-2002-X

Creative Worship Ideas

Help your teenagers discover the joy of participating in meaningful worship with 70 great ideas! You get the best ideas from youth workers across the country—ideas they've tested and that work!

ISBN 1-55945-099-1

The Group Songbook

Here's the complete music resource kit for youth groups. Packed with over 100 of the songs kids like best, it includes everything from contemporary Christian hits to traditional favorites. The accompaniment book comes with piano scores and guitar chords, plus fun and creative song-leading ideas to make group singing a success.

Accompaniment Book	ISBN 1-55945-071-1
Lyrics Book	ISBN 1-55945-049-5
Lyrics Transparencies	ISBN 1-55945-087-8

Split-Channel Cassettes and Compact Discs

Cassette, Vol. 1	ISBN 1-55945-136-X	Compact Disc, Vol. 1	ISBN 1-55945-153-X
Cassette, Vol. 2	ISBN 1-55945-088-6	Compact Disc, Vol. 2	ISBN 1-55945-089-4
Cassette, Vol. 3	ISBN 1-55945-166-1	Compact Disc, Vol. 3	ISBN 1-55945-167-X

Group's Praise & Worship Songbook

These fresh arrangements of 70 favorite praise and worship songs will add new life to any youth group or adult worship experience!

Accompaniment Book	ISBN 1-55945-268-4
Lyrics Book	ISBN 1-55945-269-2
Lyrics Transparencies	ISBN 1-55945-270-6

Split-Channel Cassettes and Compact Discs

Cassette, Vol. 1	ISBN 1-55945-251-X	Compact Disc, Vol. 1	ISBN 1-55945-253-6
Cassette, Vol. 2	ISBN 1-55945-950-6	Compact Disc, Vol. 2	ISBN 1-55945-453-9
Cassette, Vol. 3	ISBN 1-55945-450-4	Compact Disc, Vol. 3	ISBN 1-55945-452-0
Cassette, Vol. 4	ISBN 1-55945-451-2	Compact Disc, Vol. 4	ISBN 1-55945-454-7

Order today from your local Christian bookstore, or write: Group Publishing, P.O. Box 485, Loveland, CO 80539.